INTELLECT
VS
INTELLIGENCE

Regain the missing piece in your life.

SANTOSH NAMBIAR

a Life a Meditation publication

Intellect vs Intelligence

Regain the missing piece in your life.

a *Life a Meditation* publication

www.lifeameditation.com

2017

forgive me for all my ignorance

Also from the same author:

A New Way of Living: One simple step to a life without fear
Published by Balboa Press (Hay House, USA), 2012.
Life a Meditation: Practical pointers to Presence >Space > Peace
Published by LM publications, Australia, 2015.
Is this it? Taking your life from Mediocrity to Creativity
Published by LM publications, Australia 2016

To order books: www.lifeameditation.com

Dedication

You may describe it in words, you may analyse it, and you may try to understand it.
You may try to argue about it, you may like or dislike it, you may have an opinion about it. Yet that's not it.

You can be it. You are it.

And when you are it, you will know it. Only you will know it.

When you try to describe it, you are not it.

I dedicate this book to that Spaciousness (Oneness).

This book may be ordered through a bookseller or by contacting:
Life a Meditation
www.lifeameditation.com
info@lifeameditation.com

The author of this book does not dispense medical advice or prescribe the use of any technique as a form of treatment for physical, emotional, or medical problems without the advice of a physician, either directly or indirectly. The intent of the author is only to offer information of a general nature to help you in your quest for emotional and spiritual well-being. In the event you use any of the information in this book for yourself, which is your constitutional right, the author and the publisher assume no responsibility for your actions.

Any people depicted in imagery are models, and such images are being used for illustrative purposes only.

Printed in the United States of America
Date: 01/11/2017

Have you ever had the good fortune to observe the face of a young child? Have you noticed the joy emanating from her or his face? The innocence shining from the body? The natural warmth, joy and love? It's amazing how the simple look on the face of a child can make us forget our worries instantly. Let us not forget that we were all once full of joy and innocence, as children are.

When did the joy disappear from our faces? Why is there so much anger, fear, stress, sorrow and anxiety in us today as adults? What changed during our transition from childhood to adulthood? Was it our upbringing? Has society shaped who we are today?

We were, as babies, pure, uncorrupted, unconditioned, true, innocent, selfless beings. That is our primordial nature. That is our home where we belong effortlessly. As we grow up, we wander away from our home. We are conditioned; we become selfish. We are divided. There is anger, fear, the feeling of loneliness, and the feeling of being incomplete and lost. We do not know the path back to our own home. We struggle.

It's time to get back home. Home, where we truly belong.

Contents

Foreword

It's wonderful to connect with people in the world who are intent on forging a path for others to become more awake and aware and live more wholeheartedly. My dear friend, Santosh, has done just this with this book. Rather than relying on academic jargon or ancient esoteric terms, this highly accessible guide offers clear, simple, practical pointers to enjoying a more conscious, creative and expansive life. A life which is full of space and peace and joy—a space which we enjoyed as very young children. To achieve this, Santosh encourages us to rediscover a beginner's mind and a child's wonder. He encourages us to tighten our hold on the things we have learned and to which we are attached and to start to observe the mind's incessant chatter. To become more intimately aware of sensations, feelings, and thoughts—and amongst all of these experiences—to start noticing the gap, the pause, the space in every moment.

As the fifteenth century astrologer and physician of the soul Marsilio Ficino recommended, we need to turn toward the mystery of our own nature the way a sunflower turns towards the sun. Indeed, in this book In between thoughts, Santosh encourages us to become fascinated with our existence and to ask questions about the way we are choosing to live. "Is this it?", for example.

This is a wonderful, highly practical text. As a Yoga teacher with over two decades of experience, I feel that it contains valuable teachings on how to live a more conscious life and how to maximise one's full creative potential.

Thank you Santosh for this terrific offering!

 Fiona x

Fiona Hyde

Principal – Williamstown Yoga & Meditation

Williamstown

Australia

What prompted me to pen this book?

When we are born, we possess a natural abundance of joy and happiness. Our brains are fresh and pure. We are one with the world, full of vitality and beauty. We are full of joy, and observe the world with awe and wonderment. However, around the age of two or three, we come to understand that we are separate from other people and our surroundings. How does this happen?

As young children, we continue to rely on parents, teachers and the rest of society to instruct us on what to say and do. They tell us what is good for us, which school to attend, what clothing to wear, how to behave, and so on. We quickly learn that in order to survive, we must conform to whatever our parents, teachers, and other adults say, or risk being labeled disobedient and then punished. Parents pass on their experiences, knowledge, conditioning, and culture—dead, second-hand, outdated information—expecting us to preserve these old traditions and ancient beliefs. We dutifully record every bit of this knowledge in our brains and develop our identities and an image of who we are ('my -self') based on it. In this process, the joy and happiness we innately experienced as infants give way to anger, jealousy and 'self'-centeredness. As we get older, we give up and blindly accept whatever knowledge our authority figures have taught us. When this doesn't work and we are unable to cope with life's innumerable problems, we begin to struggle.

My life today is not the same as it was when I was a young child. Things that were beautiful and amazing to me then no longer seem that way. Could it be that I have already imprinted in my brain pictures of the world's wonders—the sky and its innumerable stars, the majestic mountains, valleys, and the vast oceans—so I don't need to look at them again to be reminded of their beauty? When I do occasionally take a break from monotonous adult life to observe and enjoy the beauty around me, I feel immensely happy, but real life quickly beckons me back to the "battle." I find that taking time off from the battlefield of life becomes monotonous after a few days and I am eager to get back to work again. Why does the beauty around me become a thing of joy for only short periods? Have I become so used to the mechanical routine of day-to-day life that I am unable to venture away from it for long? How did I get to be this way?

Growing up, I relied on parents and teachers to tell me what to do, how to behave, and to observe, follow, and imitate the so-called "successful" people around me. Trusting that they knew what was best for me, I always obeyed them. I became convinced that I was incapable of making any meaningful decisions for myself. I adopted this "roadmap" to my life that was created and handed to me, never for a moment questioning it or realising that I had merely borrowed it from others. As I grew older, I tried very hard to conform to this borrowed road map, even though it clearly didn't help me to meet life's challenges. My great achievements in life became part of the extra "baggage" I carried in a futile attempt to find happiness. Along with the tangible baggage like my bank balance, house, furniture, paintings, education, and so on, I also carried fear, sorrow, unhappiness, jealousy, envy, frustration and anger. My attempts to escape this fear, anger and sorrow and seek happiness, joy and a peaceful state of mind were always unsuccessful.

From an early age, I was taught that if I was armed with the right education, I could accomplish just about anything in life. Knowledge reigned supreme, according to my parents and teachers. It was the perfect tool with which to manoeuvre through the treacherous journey of life—and the more the better. Life was a battlefield, and if I didn't possess the right intellectual tools, I would lose the war to smarter people who could outwit me. Around every corner something or somebody would be lurking, waiting to defeat me; therefore, I would need to be cautious of every step I took, always alert and armed with sufficient knowledge to defend myself. To avoid being left behind, I would need to keep up with those around me who were accumulating vast amounts of knowledge. In order to succeed in life and be respected, I had to have a strong educational foundation, and the fastest way to get this was to attend university and obtain a degree.

After earning a university degree and arming myself with a vast amount of knowledge, I found that I was able to meet life's challenges with some degree of confidence. However, despite all the knowledge and experience I had gained, I realised that most people were still not interested in my beliefs or opinions. Over time, I came to discover the reasons for this:

1. All our opinions and beliefs are based on previous knowledge and experiences stored in our brain cells in the form of memories. For example, we like or dislike something to the extent that we have had a prior experience of it.

2. It is the role of our 'self'—an image or an identity we have created for ourselves in life (we can call it ego)—to staunchly protect and defend these beliefs and opinions without question. When someone offers an opinion that may or may not conform to ours, we only pretend to listen to his or her views, while our brain continually

searches the vast database in its memory bank for references and data to support our own convictions.

Eventually, I came to the conclusion that my road map of previous knowledge would never lead me down the path to joy; in fact, it would only hold me back. My choice was simple but not easy. Would I continue carrying the baggage of the 'self' and leading the same old life of conflict, struggle, frustration, anxiety, emptiness and confusion, or let go of all this baggage so I could live a life of everlasting joy? I had always been told that that sorrow, anger and pain were part of life, and I had become so attached to my baggage I didn't think I could live without it. How could I possibly dispose of the baggage I had so painstakingly collected and carried all my life? Who would I be without my baggage? Would people respect me without it? Would they even recognise me? Would I be lonely?

Most of us don't stop to ask these questions. We don't realise that it's possible to change the course of our lives. We are scared to try something new. We think we are destined to lead the mechanical life we inherited from our parents and grandparents. We grow up, get married, start a family and strive for success and power, only to experience jealousy, envy, fear, frustration and unhappiness. We wonder why we don't feel whole, and hope and pray that something or someone will "complete" us at some point in the future. Every moment of our lives we struggle to find ourselves. We seek out friends, teachers, and society for answers to our problems and become dependent upon them to fix our troubles. We have been programmed to ignore our own brains and instead listen to people who supposedly have immense knowledge and education.

Because we don't know how to think for ourselves, we become trapped in a prison created by our parents and their ancestors. This prison soon becomes familiar to us; we feel at home there. We decorate the walls with our achievements in life—degrees, accolades, status symbols—to make us believe we are happy, but this happiness is temporary and unfulfilling at best. We feel a need to protect ourselves from others, which makes us feel separate and alone. We get caught in the grip of desire. We strive to achieve things in life and then become attached to those achievements— power, status, material possessions, and so on. The "thought" of losing what we have achieved causes us great anxiety and fear. We are unhappy and occasionally feel the urge to escape the prison, only to quickly slip back into its familiar confines.

It never occurs to us that the answer to our struggle may be inside us, within our brain; that our outdated thoughts, past conditioning and beliefs might be the real cause of our conflict, fear and frustration in life. We never question the validity of the second-hand knowledge stored within our brains. Is it possible that this knowledge we work so hard to acquire and protect is actually preventing us from fully functioning in society? Preventing us from fully flowering? Why have our attempts to find an alternate way of living been so unsuccessful? Why have we been unable to make this shift? Are we waiting for someone to show us the way? Is it even possible to create such a life for ourselves?

In the next few chapters, I am going to share with you the trials and tribulations that led me on the journey of self-realisation or self-discovery. A journey that is still continuing even at this moment as you read this book. A journey to constantly recognize and perhaps cleanse myself of all that unwanted baggage and conditioning that I acquired during my upbringing, which then will allow me to lead a life free from it. Is such a life possible? Let us find out for ourselves.

Preface

Like most of us, I began my journey in life with the desire to achieve and accumulate—a 'successful' position in society, a prestigious job, power, money, a top-of-the-range car and a house in an affluent suburb (just to name a few). Yet unbeknownst to me at the time, in the process I also accumulated anger, fear, an overbearing ego, arrogance and jealousy. I did not care about the sensitivities of people around me. I was happy as long as I achieved what I set out to do, which often involved confronting and competing with others.

In early 2002, I was diagnosed with a serious illness and went through a period of intense suffering. I met death face-to-face. The U-turn (or may I say awakening) occurred at that moment. My priorities got realigned. My life became one of giving, forgiving, loving and being compassionate. I wanted to learn more about life— why do most of us struggle in life? Why are most of us sad, full of sorrow and leading a mediocre life? Thus began my self-inquiry.

I began to observe and notice my thoughts—how my thoughts continuously moved from the past through the present into the future. I became much more attentive and alert and observed my thoughts moment to moment. I would observe my fear, anger, stress and other emotions as and when they arose. And I came to understand that these emotions were the outcome of the movement of my thoughts. I also discovered that the moment I observed a thought, the thought activity would cease and there would be space. And this space was filled with peace, silence, stillness and great creativity.

I now have a new lease on life, so precious, which I cherish moment to moment. My life is filled with space. The realisation or awareness of this space, and the full experiencing of this space, can liberate you from past conditioning and baggage containing fear, anger, anxiety, self-centeredness, jealousy and so forth—qualities and emotions that you have most likely allowed to run your life thus far. When you get in touch with this space, this awareness enables you to let go of past conditioning, bringing about a completely new awareness of yourself and the world—an awareness that is very different from what you have ever known. For the first time, you are able to see beyond the 'limited' self and limited mental conditioning. Instead of observing and judging through filters of the past, you can begin to view every moment in the present, where there is no 'self' and 'no desire to acquire'. No longer encumbered by anger, fear, frustration, anxiety and jealousy, you can then begin to experience a life of freedom, joy, beauty compassion, intelligence, love and wholeness.

It can happen only in the 'Now' when the activity of the mind ceases.

As a human being, you have a choice: a choice to live a life filled with fear, anxiety, sorrow, anger, arrogance, ego and struggle or a life filled with compassion, joy, benevolence, freedom and beauty. The choice is yours. This choice is available to you NOW.

Santosh Nambiar
Melbourne, Australia

Introduction

Before you proceed any further with this book, may I ask you a question? There must have been some reason for you to have picked up this book. You could have chosen a thriller, a fiction novel or a self-help book. Why this book? Is there something bothering you in life? Like, for example, a feeling of being incomplete, despite having achieved much in life and continuing to do so? Or perhaps you feel lonely? Anger, fear, anxiety, stress, hatred, jealousy and violence are so common in our society these days. Does this bother you? Are you overwhelmed with fear?

Is fear keeping you trapped, preventing you from fully functioning in society? Peace of mind? Is this a challenge for you in the chaotic world we live in today? We all live with various challenges like this day in and day out, don't we? Do you feel stuck?

Fear, anger, hatred, jealousy, anxiety, stress, and lack of peace may all just be the end result of our combined actions. So, what is the root cause of these problems? In other words, if we understand fear and anger and so forth to be like the branches of a tree, we need to discover the root of the 'tree' to take care of the branches. If we continue to trim the branches without understanding the root cause, we may continue to suffer.

So, what is the root cause of your problems in life?

If you were to endeavor to find a way to eliminate fear, anger, stress, anxiety and so on, one by one, this may take an entire lifetime. This does not sound entirely appealing to me. Therefore, my question is, is it possible to end this mediocre, mechanical and unmindful life filled with fear, anger, stress, and anxiety, all at once, now, in this moment, once and for all? Is a life of joy, freedom, creativity, compassion and love possible now, in this lifetime, in this moment? Together, let us explore this further.

Who is this book written for?

I must admit that I didn't set out to write this book for a particular audience. Rather, I allowed the natural intelligence to 'push the pen', or in the case these days, 'press the keys on my keyboard'…

This book has not come from my 'intellect', but rather from a profound unlimited source of knowing. As such, please allow me to put the book out 'there' and have faith that who is meant to pick it up, will. However, I do believe that we can loosely categorise people in three ways—and my feelings are that this book may appeal particularly to those of you who fall in the first two of the following three categories:

The first category of people includes those who have little or no idea whatsoever that a life free from anger, anxiety, stress, fear and struggle is possible. Instead, individuals in this category believe that this way of mechanical/mediocre/unmindful living is 'normal', just 'part of life', and that they are stuck with it until they die. "Shit happens", and then you die…

Second are those individuals who, via intense suffering or some challenging life experience, know that a life free from struggle does exist and that they do have a choice to some extent—a choice to live a life mindfully, free from worry and struggle. This group tends to crave theoretical knowledge, immersing themselves in self-help books and attending any number of self-help workshops, public talks and intensives, and then spending countless hours analysing and interpreting the information. However, most of these individuals are stuck at the level of the 'intellect' and the 'play of words' and they struggle when it comes to putting theory into practice in their daily lives. Therefore, the second category of individuals are only slightly dissimilar to the first.

The third category consists of those individuals who do not try to understand, analyse or interpret their lives and experiences. They are fully aware that they are much more than just the sum total of their mind and intellect. Rather, these individuals pave the way for 'intelligence', or in other words, 'profound knowing' to act through them. They live a life of presence—otherwise known as mindful conscious living—every moment of their lives. In my view, these are the individuals who are able to truly live a life free from anger, fear, stress, anxiety and struggle, and instead, experience constant joy, beauty, oneness, compassion and freedom. These beings bloom, flower and spread their fragrance far and wide, yet usually prefer to remain anonymous and have no interest in seeking fame and glory. This category of individuals do not need to read this book. They are already living it.

Notes before you read this book:

Please note that this book has several typographical errors, grammatical mistakes and some repetition. I have also deviated from the norms and conventions of a normal book layout. This has been done deliberately with an intention to make you aware or mindful of your conditioned thoughts and judgments that come up in your mind on seeing these unusual mistakes. Just observe those thoughts that come up in your mind on seeing the mistakes, repetition and deviations from the norms and conventions. You will feel like correcting them, judging and making remarks about the mistakes. Just observe those judgments and thought movements. Rather than reacting... be an observer without any comments... You are now entering a different realm altogether... Now read on...

The jumbled array of words may not make sense to the mind. When that mind that is always judging and making comment is silent, in that silence, these words and sentences might point you to that truth that you are seeking. One of these words or sentences might get you to that 'Ah-moment' that you have been waiting for.

Why are we unmindful in life?

Mindfulness—commonly known as meditation—is the most talked about word everywhere in the world. Many workshops, seminars and lectures attempt to unravel the concept hidden in this mystical word. Even the corporates, the defence force and prison officers and inmates practice mindfulness to bring some kind of peace and order to the chaotic lives that we lead today.

The question then arises—why are we unmindful in life?

I am reminded of an incident that I witnessed when I was filling up my car at a petrol station near where I live.

I noticed a young man filling up his car with fuel. He was constantly looking at his phone as he was filling up the car. He finished filling up and went to the counter to pay. He was looking at his phone and obviously trying to read an email or Facebook post as he walked to the counter. At the counter, he did not make eye contact with the person serving at the counter. The person at the counter looked at me and smiled. The person at the counter was in a good mood. He had a good sense of humour. He asked the young man who was looking at his phone if he was interested in the special for the day. He added that there was a good offer on the mints. The young man, without lifting his eyes from the phone, said, "no". The person at the counter asked him if he wanted the receipt. He said, "no". The person at the counter looked at me briefly with a wink in his eyes and asked the young man if he would like the change back, to which the young man replied, "no". For a moment, the young man woke up and realised what he had just said. "Sorry, yes I want the change back." The person at the counter smiled at me and I smiled back. Most of the time we are unmindful. We do things mechanically.

When you are driving home from work, you are at the wheel, you are driving, and at the same time, you are either thinking about the meeting that you had that afternoon or the meeting scheduled for tomorrow. You may also have the radio on to give you some company. You may not listen actively to the radio as you are thinking and driving at the same time. There may be passive listening. No wonder that when you get home, you don't even remember how you got home.

We are unmindful, aren't we? Is that why most of our actions in life are at best mediocre and just mechanical? We just get by. There is a feeling of being incomplete in life. Despite achieving many things in life, we feel incomplete. There is something missing. What is it?

We seldom live in the moment. Every moment is a stepping stone to the next moment, and the next, and so on. This moment eludes us as we are constantly searching for a better moment.

Is it possible for us to be rooted in this moment? Is it possible for us to be mindful of everything that we are doing? Can we move from that unconsciousness to being conscious, or unmindfulness to being mindful? Or are we destined to lead a mechanical, unmindful and mediocre life? Let us find out more in the next few chapters.

Three cornerstones:

There are three very important cornerstones that you need to be mindful or aware of in order to pave way for this profound knowing to happen in you:

1. Whatever I am going to say or write in this book is nothing new. Many have already known about this, written about this and spoken about it several centuries ago. If you are reading this book with an intention of knowing something new, you may be disappointed. I will explain why a bit later.

2. You cannot grasp this with your mind. When you do, you will elude it. We always try to get a handle on everything with our mind. Unfortunately, this so-called truth or profound knowing that you are seeking will elude you if you attempt to grasp it with your mind. When the mind is quiet, this profound knowing will come to you.

3. There is no shortcut to knowing this. If you are reading this book or any other book to get a shortcut to knowing this, you will be disappointed. You need what I call all the four D's:
Dedication
Determination
Devotion
Discipline

If you are someone who says that you will go to gym tomorrow morning at 9 o'clock and then you do, then you can do this.

Please be aware and mindful of these three most important cornerstones as you read this book.

What makes mindfulness a concept so difficult for us to understand?

It seems that the concept behind mindfulness—commonly known as meditation—is very confusing, complicated and riddled with mysticism. It is most often associated with spirituality.

There has been a lot written about meditation since time immemorial. Ancient Indian scriptures are full of it. Jesus has spoken about it, and so has Buddha. Quran and Bhagavad Gita talk about it in great detail. People are continuing to write about it and talk about it even today. There are several books and techniques in the market telling you what to do. There are workshops and seminars on it happening all around the world right now as you read this book. Many will continue to speak about it even after we die.

So, many people have said many things about it. Is that then perhaps why it is confusing and complicated? It seems we don't know what is right or what is wrong. Our brain is cluttered with the knowing from these many sources. Is this right? Is that, right? What did he say? What did she say? Who to follow? Confusing, isn't it? We seem to grapple with it yet not get anywhere.

Let me ask you a question, may I? I have already mentioned that mindfulness or meditation as a concept is nothing new. Many people have written about mindfulness in the past, and many continue to write about it even today. So, my question is, why haven't you got it? What prevented you from knowing about mindfulness? Why has this valuable information eluded you? Good question, you may say.

But let us leave this question aside for a moment and come back to it a bit later.

As you read this book, you are comfortably seated on a chair. Your physical body is on a chair. Now, for a moment, turn your attention to your head. What's happening in your head as you read this book? What's happening to your mind? It's constantly wandering, isn't it? It may be asking questions or making all sorts of judgments. What is this book all about? Am I wasting my precious time reading it? Will I get something out of this? What is the author talking about? I wish I could get a handle on this as soon as possible. You may even be thinking about something that happened in the past. The movie you watched, the concert you went to last night or the conversation you had with your friend last evening. You may be thinking something about the future—perhaps about the meeting you have planned for the following day. You may be thinking about your children or about your elderly parents. Wondering how they are doing. All happening all at once as you attempt to read this book. Images or scenes from the past or future constantly being projected onto a screen within our head. In other words, we are constantly thinking about past events or thinking about future events, and are never in this present moment.

For a moment, observe this constant, incessant thought activity—the mind traffic, the mind chatter, the compulsive thinking—the mind moving back into the past and future like a pendulum. Your mind is full. Is it not? We are mostly unaware or unmindful of this mind movement. This incessant thought activity is preventing us from fully knowing what I call the truth, or profound knowing. You were either in the past or in the future, but never in this present moment, and therefore this truth has eluded you.

When the pendulum-like mind activity comes to a standstill—in other words, when you are in the present, when your mind chatter comes to a standstill, and your mind is silent—in that silence, this profound knowing will come to you. The truth will be revealed, with clarity. When you are either in the past or the future (as we are for most of our lives), this will elude you.

So, to have some clarity of knowing, our incessant thought activity should come to a standstill. The confusion and clutter will then be gone, and there will be clarity, creativity, freedom, joy, love and compassion. All happening when we are in the present. The right answers will come to you at the right time.

You cannot understand mindfulness with your mind. If you attempt it, it will elude you.

Going deeper into mindfulness:

In order for us explore mindfulness a little further, let us ask ourselves some more questions.

Why are we constantly thinking? Why is our mind full with thoughts? Why is our mind constantly moving back and forth like a pendulum?

What are thoughts?

What effect does thought activity or constant thinking have on our body?

If thoughts or compulsive thinking have such a detrimental effect on our body, how can we bring this thought activity to an end?

Let us see if we can throw some light on these questions and bring some clarity in the next few chapters.

Let us take up the question—what effect does thought have on our body?

Some of you may be going to the gym to exercise and keep your body fit. Many do other kinds of physical exercise, like going for a jog or a swim, riding a bike, doing Zumba, and so on. These activities are all very good and keep us physically fit. But what about mentally? Our mind is constantly wandering and creating chaos in our lives. Most of us do not think about the harm this thought activity is causing our physical body. But we do not have control over our mind. Or do we?

Let us turn our attention to our physical body. What is it made of? How does it come into being? The egg and the sperm fertilise to form a single-celled organism called a 'zygote'. This single cell divides several times to form over 10 trillion cells. Out of these 10 trillion cells, several million cells form your organs, like your lungs, heart, liver, and kidney and so on. Therefore, your body and your organs are nothing but a bundle of several trillion tiny cells. They are all working together and talking to each other as a team to perform various functions in the body—functions such as digestion, breathing, absorption of nutrients—to keep us alive.

Let us say you are thinking. Thinking, perhaps, about the meeting or job interview or exam scheduled for tomorrow. When you are thinking, you are sending a stress signal from the brain to various parts of the body via a network of neurons. These signals (stress, anger, fear, anxiety) put a lot of stress on the 10 trillion cells that make up the organs in your body. The organs are constantly under the pump. How long can the organs take this stress?

There is generally a threshold beyond which the cells and organs give up and say, "I can't handle this stress anymore". Now you end up in a state called dis-ease. The cells are not at ease with each other. They are unable to perform their function. This creates a lot of stress on your physical wellbeing.

Constant compulsive thinking can cause your body a lot of harm. However, we are mostly unaware of it and take it for granted that such thinking is part of life.

But if these thoughts have such a detrimental effect on the body, don't we need to sit up and take notice of them? See if we can overcome them, to safeguard and protect our own body before it succumbs to disease, deterioration and death?

Self-realisation or self-discovery

Before we attempt to answer the remaining questions about thoughts and why we constantly think, we may need to dive deep within ourselves and ask some more questions. A kind of re- discovering of our own self. In other words, we may need to ask ourselves, who am I, really?

We should have done this self-discovery a long time ago. However, since we are constantly on the treadmill of life, we may not have had the time to sit back and ponder it. Let us do it now before it's too late.

We are born, we grow up, we get an education, a degree and a job, buy a house or two, build a bank balance, get married, have children, and seek happiness through our children—only to find that when they grow up, they no longer need us, and then we feel lonely and depressed.

During this so-called metamorphosis, we accumulate a lot of anger, fear, anxiety, jealousy and stress.

Finally, it's time to die. A life so mediocre! Don't we need to ask the question, is this it? Really? Who am I? What is my purpose in life? Let us dive deep within ourselves in an attempt to find an answer. Let us do the self-discovery now.

But hang on, there is another important thing to consider. When you do this self-discovery and when you ask these questions, where is the answer coming from? Is it not coming from knowledge that has been acquired from our teachers, our parents, the computer, the many books we have read, and our own experience of the past? Let us for a moment put aside that acquired knowledge and instead use our own brain to seek the answers to our questions.

We do not want the answers that we have already acquired from various sources interfering with our self-inquiry. We do not want borrowed answers. Let us therefore say, "I don't know, but I am going to find out for myself". When we say "I don't know", we pave the way for further knowing to happen. This knowing will not be from the knowledge previously borrowed or acquired, but rather, it will come through using our own brain—the uncluttered brain—to find the solutions and answers to the challenges that we face today.

Imagine a sponge that has completely soaked up water. Can it absorb more water? Perhaps not. Similarly, our brain is cluttered with what others have said—knowledge acquired from various sources. We need to squeeze the sponge thoroughly in order for it to absorb more water.

Let us therefore take a clean sheet of paper and start our own self-discovery, inquiry, or self-realisation.

Now let us ask some more questions as we slowly get into the self-discovery, shall we?

What are some of the challenges that we facing in our current life situations? What are the challenges or hurdles that prevent us from fully functioning in our society? Things like, for example, 'fear'.

Fear keeps us bottled up and prevents us from fully functioning in society, does it not? We take one step forward and two steps back.

What other hurdles or challenges come to your mind that prevent you from fully flowering in life. Anger? There is so much anger in all of us. Anger creates a barrier between us and others around us.

Stress, anxiety, loneliness, and a feeling of being incomplete in life —let us put them together on a white sheet of paper.

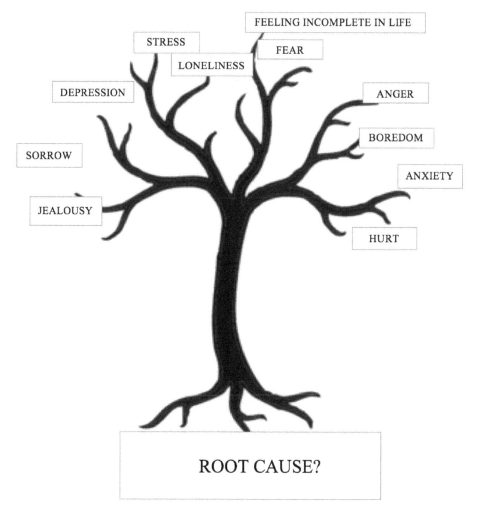

Imagine those roadblocks, hurdles or challenges to be the branches a large tree. There is a root cause of all these problems we are facing in life. Anger, fear, jealousy, anxiety, stress, loneliness are all just the side effects. What is the root cause of all these problems?

Let us dive deep within and find out for ourselves. If we are able to find out the root cause and work on it, we may be able to get rid of the effects once and for all. We don't need to work on anger, fear, and anxiety and stress one by one. Instead, let's just work on the root cause. After all, if we do not work on the root cause, we are just trimming the branches and will continue to do so throughout our lives, thus continuing to suffer anger, fear and stress. However, if we are able to get to the root of the problem, we can be free from all that suffering once and for all. Free from fear, anger, and stress, so that we are able to fully flower and function as a human being in society.

There will be a lot more clarity in our life once our past baggage is all gone. The clutter and confusion will no longer be there. It will be as if a veil has been lifted. The veil of confusion—the veil of clutter —will be gone. We will be able to see clearly, listen clearly, and— for the first time—experience the spectacle of nature all around us. View life without those glasses that we have put on, thus seeing the REALITY and realising the TRUTH for the first time. It will be as if we have come out of the prison that we have created for ourselves. Freedom, joy, clarity, creativity, compassion and benevolence will prevail in our life.

A life free from fear, anger, anxiety and stress is possible. We don't have to live with it and suffer.

So, what is the root cause of all our challenges in our life? Let's find out as we go a little bit deeper into our self-discovery.

I invite you to close your eyes and sit quietly for a minute or two. I realise I may be asking you to do something next to impossible. You may be able to climb a mountain, or run a marathon, but sitting quietly even for a minute may not be your cup of tea. Just give it a go and let us see what happens…

Were you aware of the beautiful silence on the outside? Perhaps the occasional hum of the air-conditioner, a bird singing or a car driving by? Or perhaps you were aware of perfect silence.

What about your inner world? Did you experience silence on the inside? Or perhaps you noticed a lot of noise. Your mind full of thoughts… one after another. Incessant thought activity. Were you aware of this thought activity? Perhaps not, because on average, we have 48 thoughts per minute and approximately 80,000 thoughts per day.

Therefore, if you sat quietly for, let's say, three minutes, you may have had approximately 144 thoughts. These thoughts may have consisted of things like: what's my plan for the evening? What's for dinner tonight? Do I have to pick up the children tonight? When is my next meeting? Will I get to keep my job? What shall we plan for the weekend? What am I doing here with my eyes closed and doing nothing when I have several things on my list of things to do which I need to complete for the day? One thought after another...

A MIND FULL

You may be completely unaware of this thought activity happening in your head because you have become accustomed to living this way. Yet if this is the case, with that kind of thought activity—or shall we say, mental traffic—in your head, how can you read a book like this with 'undivided' attention? How can you listen to what others are saying or truly see the world outside of yourself? So it becomes like a parallel world. You living with your thoughts on the inside, while the world outside passes by without you perhaps even noticing it.

Every moment of your existence, you are engaged in acting and reacting to the thoughts in your head. And every thought tells you, "I am important, so you better take care of me otherwise you'll get into trouble."

Your thoughts keep you on a constant treadmill, and you continue to act and react to each and every thought. Each thought vies for your attention. You are therefore generally anxious, stressed, living in fear, anger and so on. As a result, you seldom see, hear or listen to anything happening on the outside—or rather, you only have partial attention on things outside of yourself. As such, you fail to see the beauty of nature contained within the external world—flowers blooming, birds singing, and the spectacle of nature dancing before you. Instead, all go unnoticed. All due to the incessant thought activity in your head.

Wouldn't it be nice to have some respite from the incessant thoughts, confusion and clutter in your head whilst reading this book?

Don't we all need some space and peace from the constant mental commentary in our heads to understand what is contained in any book in order to appreciate what the author is trying to say?

Thoughts? So, what are these thoughts? What do they consist of? Let's continue exploring what they are…

What are thoughts?

Thoughts, what are they? Have you thought about it?

In order to understand how thoughts are created, let us imagine a situation. You have gone to an ice cream shop. You had a fantastic ice cream. You enjoyed the taste and flavour and, overall, had a pleasant experience at the shop. The next time you think of enjoying an ice cream, the first thought that comes to your mind is the experience you had at the ice cream shop the other day, where you enjoyed that great tasting ice cream. How did this happen? The taste, the flavour and the overall experience are already stored in your brain. Your mind moves back in time and retrieves the experience and information stored in the brain, and projects it into the future. "I wish I had that ice cream, the ice cream that I tasted at the shop the other day." The whole experience replays in your head. The taste, the flavour, and the atmosphere in the shop…these memories flash across the movie screen in your head.

If, for some reason, you don't get the same ice cream that you remembered from last time, there's a good chance you'll be unhappy and grumpy this time, isn't there? This is how your 'likes' and 'dislikes' come into being. It's as if your 'likes' and 'dislikes' are wired for life like the neurons wired in the brain. All our 'likes', 'dislikes' and 'opinions' are based on previous knowledge and experience stored in our brain in the form of memories. We 'like' or 'dislike' something to the extent we have had a prior experience of it.

Thoughts can therefore be understood as past experiences stored in our brain in the form of memories. Our minds retrieve information and experiences from the past and then project these into the future at lightning speed. And let us remember that we have approximately 48 thoughts per minute. A multitude of retrieved images and experiences being projected forward, one after the other...

Let me give you another example from my personal life. When I was a child of around eight years old, a teacher at my school asked me to come to the front of the classroom and speak a few words about myself to the class. I hesitantly stood up and slowly walked to the front of the class. I was nervous. I was shaking with fear. Words would not come out of my mouth. My mouth was dry. I stood there in silence for several minutes unable to speak. I stared blindly at the walls of the classroom. I felt so ashamed and defeated in front of the teacher and my classmates. It was a dark feeling.

This experience of fear and embarrassment became stored in my brain. Even today when I am getting ready to speak publicly, my mind goes back in time and retrieves memories of this past experience and projects them into the future...as if to say, "... beware! You were a failure once therefore be careful." The images of the past are replayed in my head enough to send shivers down my spine.

I am sure many of you can relate to what I am describing here. Different scenarios that were past experiences continue to impact on your present life. Whether it be a previous failure in an exam or interview, fear of spiders, losing a job, losing a loved one, and so on. All these experiences are recorded and stored in our brain. Fear, anger, jealousy and stress all carefully recorded since the time we were children...till this very moment. You have recorded every moment of your life so far. It never stops.

Even now as you read this book, you are recording information in your brain. Therefore, can you imagine the amount of information that is already recorded and stored in your brain? Several terabytes of data. A separate folder for fear, anger, anxiety, stress, jealousy, anger and so forth. Perhaps the folder titled 'Anger' has several files containing instances of anger from your earliest memories till now, carefully labelled, stored and ready to recall any moment at the beck and call of your mind.

Similarly, the folders labelled 'Fear,' 'Jealousy,' 'Anxiety' and so on, most likely have numerous sub-folders and files of past experiences stored in your brain. And your mind is able to access these past experiences much faster than a super computer can. Therefore, can you imagine the clutter your brain has been carrying since childhood, and continues to carry every moment, even today? As long as there is information from the past stored in your brain in a multitude of folders and files, incessant thought activity will exist in your head. The question then becomes, is it possible for us to erase these folders—folders of fear, anger, hatred, jealousy, envy and so forth? Choosing to erase one folder—say, 'Fear'—and all the files and memories associated with it, may take several years—perhaps even a whole lifetime. At the same time, we are continually recording new fears (experiences) and storing them in the 'Fear' folder. Therefore, erasing one folder after another would most likely be an incredibly arduous task.

It may even prove to be impossible. So, are we stuck with these folders for life? Do we have to continue to live life with fear, anger, anxiety and stress, and accept these as unavoidable aspects of life? Or is it possible to erase all of the folders once and for all—now, in this lifetime, in this moment. If you don't believe it's possible to dissolve the files all at once, in this instant, it may be futile for you to read any further. But if there is a tiny part of you that believes it may be possible, and you are keen to know more, please read on. Together, let us explore further if all the combined folders of fear, anger, hatred, jealousy, hatred, and so on can be dissolved all at once —now, in this moment—allowing us to function fully in society.

Is it possible to be free from fear, anger, jealousy, arrogance, stress and anxiety?

Every thought in your head sends a signal from the brain to each of the 10 trillion cells in your body and back through a highly specialised network of neurons. These thoughts in your head are generally about the past or the future. If your thoughts concern a past incident in your life, you may be initiating a cascade of fear, anger, hatred, envy, and so forth, to the 10 trillion cells and back. If the thoughts in your head concern the future, you may be sending a signal of anxiety. Either way, your cells are constantly under the pump, reacting to various signals from the brain.

How long can your cells survive in these stressed conditions? Sooner or later, the cells will start to retaliate and you may end up with a condition called dis-ease. Surely your cells—indeed your entire bodies—are not at ease with the constant barrage of negative signals coming from the brain. As a result, your body may end up succumbing to diseases such as cancer, and perish.

Are you aware of the incessant thought activity in your head and its effect on the body? For most of us, we are conditioned to accept this constant activity and remain unaware even of its existence and impact upon us.

So thoughts move back and forth like a pendulum, retrieving PAST experiences of fear and anger, for example, and projecting these experiences and memories into the FUTURE. This often creates a great deal of anxiety, leading you to a situation where you feel constantly stressed or anxious.

THE MIND PENDULAM

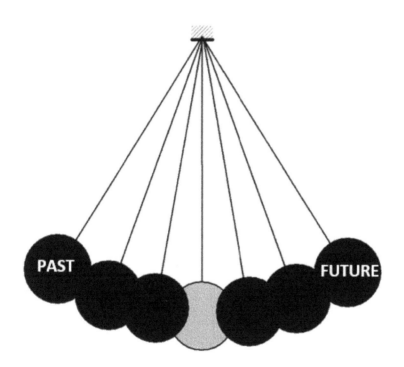

As long as there is constant movement of the pendulum, anxiety and stress will exist in your life. You will be on a treadmill all the time. Tiring, isn't it?

In order for you to slow down on the treadmill of life, you need to slow the movement of the pendulum. In other words, the thoughts going back and forth must slow down. The constant chatter in your head will need to quieten and, even better, come to an end.

In other words, you have to be in the PRESENT.

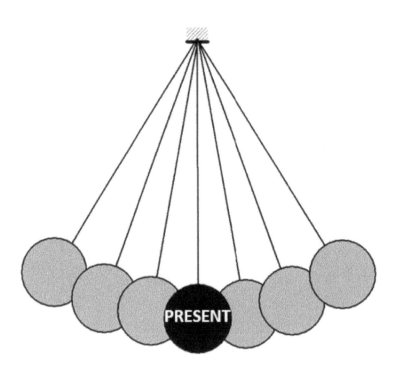

Is it possible for the thought activity to be slowed or, even better, to cease?

As mentioned earlier, your brain is constantly engaged in the thinking process. Most of the time you are unaware of the incessant 'chatter' going on in your mind because you are accustomed to it and have tuned it out. For now, try to turn your attention to your head. For the next minute or two, notice the thoughts coming and going in your head...

When you observe carefully, you will notice that although the movement of thoughts seems swift, there are gaps. A gap in which a thought comes to an end and a new thought hasn't yet appeared. For example, in the case of the ice cream mentioned earlier. You may be thinking about the ice cream you had the other day—"I wish I had the same ice cream"—and the taste and the flavour of the ice cream come into your mind. Yet if you observe closely, you notice that the previous ice cream experience comes and goes in a flash—a micro-second. Quite quickly, the memory of the ice cream comes to an end and a new thought appears. For example, "How about going to see a movie tonight? Which movie, which theatre and with whom?". In between the thought about the movie and the thought about the ice cream, there is space—a space in which you realise you have been caught up in thinking. This space or gap is not related to the thought process. We don't usually notice this space. But if you observe carefully, you will become aware that this space is one of silence. A brief space in which there is no thought—just space and silence. This space is the missing piece in your life. Not knowing that this space exists may be the root cause of all the problems in your life. Yet how does this space free us from fear, anger, stress and anxiety?

Root cause of all our problems in life

Your own thoughts give rise to fear, anger, anxiety, loneliness, stress, depression, ego, arrogance and all the other conditioned behaviours or emotions that you are experiencing.

Therefore, thoughts—or rather, incessant thought activity and therefore lack of space—may be the root cause of all your problems in life. Incessant thought activity—that is, your mind moving back into the past folders to retrieve the stored memories of fear, anger, anxiety and all the other experiences, and projecting them into the future—is the cause of all problems in your life. If you are able to bring this thought activity to a standstill in that space of peace (in that space of no thoughts all), your conditioned behaviours are dissolved all at once, simultaneously. In that moment. Freedom from fear, anger, anxiety, stress and all conditioned behaviours. There is so much joy, unconditional love, peace, freedom, creativity, clarity and benevolence when the thought activity comes to a standstill, paving the way for the space or silence to happen in you.

Therefore, the space of peace—or space of no thoughts—is the missing piece in our lives. We are consumed with thoughts, which in turn initiate our conditioned behaviours, leading to our own suffering. When there is no thought, there are no more conditioned behaviours. You have now become that child you once were. The unconditioned, uncorrupted, innocent being.

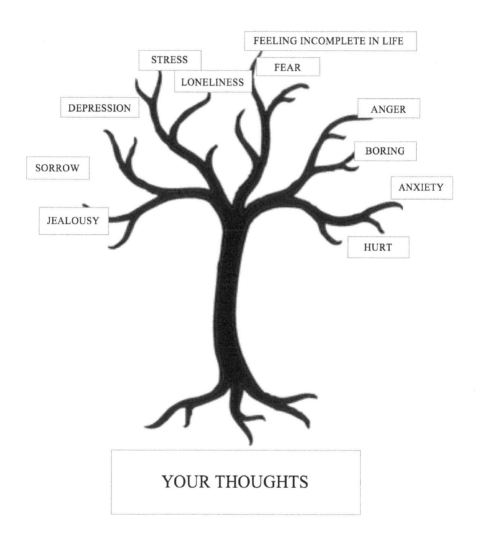

STRESS

FEELING INCOMPLETE IN LIFE

FEAR

LONELINESS

DEPRESSION

ANGER

BORING

SORROW

ANXIETY

JEALOUSY

HURT

YOUR THOUGHTS

Let us turn attention to the incessant thought activity occurring in your head. Thought after thought after thought… and yet, you may perhaps be unaware of this perpetual activity. Let us envisage this activity in your head as a long line, just like the one pictured on the next page:

▬▬▬▬▬▬▬▬▬▬▬▬▬▬▬▬▬▬

Thoughts after thoughts

Let us imagine that this long line of thoughts concerns the ice cream. As soon as you begin to observe these thoughts with all of your attention, the thoughts dissolve. The line disappears. The thoughts come to an abrupt end. At this point, we discover space. Space in which there is no thought. Initially, you may not notice the space, for it is very brief. Yet in this space there is freedom… freedom from incessant thought activity. How liberating!

In the next moment, however, a new thought emerges, for example, thoughts about going to a movie—"Which movie? Which cinema? And with whom?" Immediately, you are back again in thought activity mode, creating a new long line of thought.

Let us envisage the space between thoughts as something like the picture on the next page:

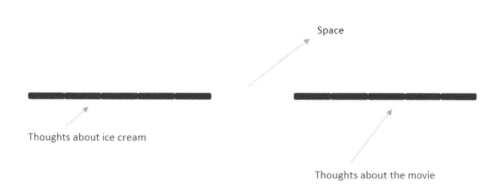

Awareness of this space—the full experiencing of this space—can liberate you from your past conditioning. It can liberate you from past baggage in which you have stored memories, including fear, anger, anxiety, self-centeredness and jealousy—memories and emotions that you have (perhaps unconsciously) allowed to run your life thus far.

In other words, by recognising and dwelling in this space for a moment, everything that has been stored in your brain from the past comes to an immediate end. Thought activity itself comes to an end. The pendulum stops right in the middle. Rather than swinging back into the past to retrieve information and experiences stored in the brain to then swing (project) forward into the future, you dwell in the present. And a momentary kind of peace and silence can be experienced in this space...

Now we need to slowly expand this space of peace in our life. More and more space and less and less of thoughts. This requires practice.

More space and less thoughts

This is where the four D's come into prominence: Dedication. Determination, Devotion and Discipline. As I mentioned earlier If you are one of those who says that I will go to gym tomorrow at 9 o'clock, and if you are the gym at 9 as promised, you can do this.

Please note that although I mentioned earlier that the several terabytes of data from the past need to be erased, this is not entirely the case. Past memories and experiences continue to remain in the brain, yet there is the understanding that they no longer need to influence (or be projected onto) our future. It's very important to note that some limited data or memory may be required for our functioning in this manifested physical world. However, we need to be mindful that this limited past memory which we have acquired and stored away is not dictating our life in the present. When that happens, the outcome may be limiting and life would be filled with the past baggage of fear, anger, stress and struggle. Therefore, we rest in the present moment—so what occurred in the past does not impact on the future. The mind pendulum is still. So, the more you can learn to dwell in the present, the less past anxiety, fear, anger or envy can affect your life or life situations.

Imagine a footpath in the forest. What happens to the path when this path has not been used for several months? Slowly, grass and other small shrubs grows over it and soon, the path has disappeared once and for all. Likewise, our default behaviour is to go back into the past to retrieve the past baggage stored in our brain to project into the future to create stress, anxiety and fear. When you are in the present, your mind is not going back into the past. That pathway is being used less and less and therefore over a period of time, this urge to go back into the past disappears.

As you learn to stay still in the present, you may also experience past experiences and memories slowly burning themselves out once and for all, as neurons are rewired and new pathways developed. With this understanding, you may ask, "Wouldn't it be great to expand this space and peace in my life?" More and more space and less and less thoughts. Is this even possible?

From my own personal experience, it is possible. You can learn to live a life of peace free from stored experiences of fear, anger, anxiety and stress. Let us envisage the expanding space as below. More space in your life and no longer one long line of incessant thought.

To Summarise: The space between Thoughts

Thoughts after thoughts

Space of no thoughts

Expanding space of no thoughts

Less and less of thoughts. More space prevails.

In this peaceful space, you dwell in the present. Your mind no longer moves back into the past to retrieve experiences, nor are experiences recorded for future reference. Rather, your mind is still and silent. The more present you are, the more space in your life. Your brain no longer records experiences as vigorously and therefore there is less internal clutter and baggage. Your brain is fresh and rejuvenated, with plenty of energy available for creative action in your life.

Continually paying attention to your thoughts and the associated background noise ensures that they will not be recorded or stored in your brain to affect your present or your future. Instead, you are now using your brain not as a store house for past information (acquired knowledge), but as a tool for accessing unlimited knowing—the abundant natural intelligence—paving the way for creative action in your life.

How can I expand this 'space of peace' in my life?

The space that we are discussing in this book, this 'space of peace', is what's really missing in most of our lives. Perhaps you feel that your life is filled with constant chatter and no space. As a result, you may find that you struggle and experience never-ending anxiety, fear, envy, anger and so forth. In order to find respite from anxiety and stress, you need to discover more of this peaceful space.

Now, the good news is—it's available to everyone.

And yet, there are no fixed paths or steps to acquiring more of this space. I cannot say, "If you follow steps 1, 2, and 3, you will reach this space". Indeed, this cannot be taught. There are, however, several pointers that lead to this space. Pointers that have worked, and continue to work, for me.

We mentioned earlier that the space between thoughts is space in which there are no thoughts. However, one of the challenges of writing a book on this topic is that this space cannot be described in words. The moment I endeavour to describe the space or add meaning to it, it is gone... because this space can never be described in words. Words come from thoughts and previous conditioning, whereas this space is beyond thoughts and conditioned knowledge.

What really happens when you try to describe the feeling of that space or try to put it in words? You have moved back into the past into your memory where the experience of that space is stored and you are describing the past experience. You are no longer in the present. Can you see the difficulty?

Imagine you have tasted honey. Can you explain your experience of the taste of the honey? You can put some words together to point to that experience. But you can never fully share with others the actual taste of honey. Can you?

Moreover, no amount of trying to understand or analyse this space will work either, because these actions arise from the conditioned mind. The space referred to here is beyond the mind, it is beyond the realm of thoughts and therefore cannot be understood in the 'normal' way of conceptualising things.

If you (your mind) desperately want to describe this space, you can attempt to describe it as a space of not knowing anything anymore and being comfortable with it. Not knowing anything anymore from the realm of the limited mind. When that mind activity stops, it paves the way for that unlimited profound knowing to happen in you.

A question may now arise in your mind. How can I live in this world without knowing and planning ahead? Will that not lead to procrastination?

When you are planning for something—say you are going on a trip in a month's time—you can plan in the present. Take the time to plan. But plan it in the present. If your thought is wandering into the future while you are planning, you are going to be anxious. Will I get the flight? Will I get the perfect accommodation? What if I don't get the visa? What if I get lost in a foreign country? See, your thoughts are wandering into the future while you are planning. This will create anxiety in you. Plan it in the present and put it away.

Imagine another situation. The time now is 4 pm in Melbourne as I write these words. Due to unforeseen circumstances, I need to catch a flight to Sydney at
10 pm. This was not planned. This trip caught me by surprise.

I have two choices.

Choice 1: I can think about all possible things that can go wrong. Like, for example, not getting a taxi on time, the traffic on the freeway, not getting a ticket, missing the flight, and so on. This is going to create panic in me and I will miss out on packing those important files and things that I need for the trip. I am going to be anxious throughout my journey.

Choice 2: Bring myself back to the present. Bring that much-wanted space in me. This means my mind is not going back into the future and thinking about all those things that can go wrong. I am rooted in the present. I am now picking up whatever is required for the meeting in Sydney. The panic is gone. I call the taxi without thinking of any consequence. I am in the taxi. I am rooted in the present. Moment to moment. Not thinking about the if's and but's of the future. I am not anxious anymore. I reach the airport and continue on my journey in the present moment to moment. Being mindful moment to moment.

What would you choose?

In summary, the expansion of this space cannot be taught—space itself cannot be described or understood—but you can BE this space. This space and peace will only come about through your own trials and tribulations. This is something very personal and is not easily shared, especially via the written word. However, I can give you some pointers to BE this space. Some pointers that I have used in my life to bring about that space in me. Pointers that will help me to remind myself to get back to the present moment.

Throughout this book, I offer several pointers, and it's important that you pick any pointers that resonate with you… that best suit you.

Many in the past—including Buddha, Jesus, Ramana Maharishi, and J. Krishnamurti— realised this space and were able to BE this space. Each, in their own way, had their own pointers to the space of peace.

You have to choose yours… your own individual pointer or pointers that will help you to BE this space. That will remind you to get back to the present moment. The space of no thoughts. The space of silence.

Some call it spaciousness. Many others call it nothingness, awareness, higher energy, consciousness, and so on. They all point to that space of no thoughts. Space of being in the present. Of being mindful.

The space of no thoughts, or space of being in the present, is our primordial state. As children, we were in that space. The space of joy. During our upbringing, we moved away from being in the present to the thought-dominated world. Thinking about past events and being anxious over some future moment, keeping us stressed, keeping us bottled up in fear. We struggle. This is our habit. Now, we need reminders or pointers to get back to our own primordial state, which is the Present moment. We need to therefore kick the habit of our constant compulsive thinking. The sooner you are able to kick the habit of compulsive thinking and be able to dwell in the present, the better it is for you. Joy, compassion, benevolence, freedom and creativity emanate from that space of no thoughts. Do you have all of the four D's (Determination, Devotion, Dedication and Discipline) to kick this habit of compulsive thinking?

When you are either in the past or future, your life is more mechanical—or may I say—unmindful. The moment you are in the present, you are more mindful. You have come alive. You are more aware, attentive and connected with everything. Connected with every other being. It's as if the veil of confusion is gone. You begin to see the reality, you begin to listen, and you begin to notice everything happening around you. There is clarity in your life. Our purpose of manifestation becomes clear to us.

To me, this space is the space of creativity. Everything creative happens only in this space. Important discoveries, paintings and great works of art, music and literature have all come into being in this silent space. When asked what inspires an individual to do such great work, you may have heard many famous artists, painters, musicians and athletes remark, "I don't know. It just happened. When I look back I didn't think I could have done it. It just happened...".

Everything happens for you in this space without struggle.

When did I lose this space?

Have you looked at a young child's face with all of your attention? The glow of joy, peace and innocence on his or her face? The goodness in them, or shall we say, the 'space' in them shines through to the external world. They are uncorrupted, unconditioned, pure, selfless beings. They have not yet been covered by the layers of conditioning and a multitude of thoughts.

Unfortunately, as children grow older, and as they begin to recognise themselves by their names, this glow (space) begins to slowly fade away. The goodness (space) in them is taken over by conditioned thoughts. Also, children begin to absorb everything from their parents, teachers, peers and surroundings. This information is stored in the brain and kept for future use. Yet this process may be likened to corrupt software (conditioning) being downloaded onto the hardware (body and brain).

Also, each child now has a 'name'—an identity (self, me and I)—and everything that they do in their lives from this point on, is to enhance this identity—developing 'likes', 'dislikes', opinions, and accumulating toys, then a bank balance and their own backyard.

The selfless being we once were has turned into a selfish or self-centred person.

All our opinions and beliefs are based on previous knowledge and experiences stored in our brain cells in the form of memories. For example, we like or dislike something to the extent that we have had a prior experience of it.

It is the role of our conceptualised 'self'—an image or an identity we have created for ourselves in life—to staunchly protect and defend these beliefs and opinions without question. When someone offers an opinion that may or may not conform to ours, we only pretend to listen to his or her views, while our brain continually searches the vast database in its memory bank for references and data to support our own convictions.

As the years go by, the thick dark layers of our conditioning (which is nothing but our mind) begin to completely cover the goodness and 'hijack' our lives. Conditioning now runs our lives instead of the goodness within us. We have also now created a barrier and separated ourselves from others around us (self and other). The 'oneness' that we once experienced as a child is lost. The space, peace, joy, freedom and innocence is replaced with arrogance, ego, anger, jealousy, hatred, stress, envy, fear, sorrow and struggle. We begin to live in that cocoon—a bubble, or shall I say, a prison—that we have created for ourselves. We suffer, we feel lonely, we struggle, we feel incomplete in life and we are unable to fully flower and thrive in society.

We're so afraid of losing our possessions, our jobs, our loved ones, our homes and our money, that we live petty, self-centred, limited, frustrated, anxious and mediocre lives, never allowing ourselves to fully flower. We are not prepared to let go of these "things"—all the experiences and memories of the past, as well as material possessions—that our thoughts have carefully put together every moment of our life. Sometimes they are so important to us that they even define our status or a concept of who we are in society with our name, fame and the material processions which ultimately gives rise to the 'self'.

So, why are we so afraid of losing what we have? Again, it all begins with our thought process. Here is how it works:

1. Our thoughts, perceptions and senses create what we desire.
2. We constantly struggle in our daily life to achieve what we desire (security, fame, money, and so on).
3. We become attached to these achievements or possessions. We fear losing what we have achieved or possessed.

The role of the 'self', or you may call it mind, is to protect us and give us a feeling of security through external, materialistic means. The self is wary and cautious, always on the lookout for anyone or anything that threatens our physical or emotional security. This creates a tremendous amount of anxiety and fear within us. Feeling separate and alone, we cling to and depend upon others to fulfil our needs. This always leads to conflict and unhappiness. As long as "the self" exists with its need to fulfil our desires, fear and conflict will remain, and intelligence and joy will be kept in abeyance. As long as we are "attached" to our possessions, achievements, and so on, the fear will never go away. As long as we blindly accept the conditioning we've received from our parents and ancestors, our lives will remain mediocre, chaotic and unfulfilling.

Frustrated with life, or perhaps out of intense suffering, we may seek to rediscover the 'space of peace'. We may read several books, delve into different spiritual philosophies, meet several spiritual teachers, meditate, go to the temples, mosques or churches, pray and hope that the peace and goodness we once experienced will return. We may believe (or hope) that 'others' can assist us to rediscover the lost sense of peace (goodness and space), not realising that the peace and goodness we had as a child remains deep within each of us. It is simply covered by several layers of conditioning (identity, thoughts, self, me and I).

In summary, this space you now seek was with you as a child. Over a period, it simply became obscured by your upbringing, conditioning and the moment you started recording everything in the brain. Anger, fear, hatred—these emotions and experiences began to fill the brain and subsequently the brain became cluttered with thoughts. Thought after thought after thought. As a result, the space eventually became obscured and the struggle began...

How can we regain that space we lost? How can we be that space of peace, like the child we were once?

As long as the dark layers of the conditioned behaviours as shown in the above picture rule our life, we are destined to struggle. How can we therefore regain that space we lost? The answer obviously is that the conditioning that we have acquired during our upbringing has to go. In other words, the conditioning has to be dissolved. How can we do this? Remember, from our self-discovery we have realised that the root cause of all conditioning, or our conditioned behaviour, is our THOUGHTS. Our thoughts give rise to the conditioned behaviours. Thoughts move back to retrieve the stored PAST experiences of fear, anger, stress, anxiety and so on, and project them into the FUTURE. This creates anxiety, stress, fear, anger, loneliness and so on. If we were in the PRESENT, our thoughts would not move back into the PAST and therefore could not retrieve the past conditioned behaviours. In other words, in the Present, when there is no movement of thought, in that space of silence, we are free of all our conditioned behaviours.

As long as you are in the present, there is no thought. When there is no thought, your baggage of conditioned behaviours (anger, anxiety, stress, fear, and so on) are dissolved all at once.

To summarise, thought gives rise to your conditioned baggage (the dark layers in the picture). When there are no thoughts in you—in other words—when you are in the present, your conditioned baggage is dissolved once and for all. Freedom from those dark layers of prison. You have emerged from that cocoon. You have now regained that lost space. Joy, compassion, creativity, clarity and unconditional love begin to express themselves.

The selfless, pure uncorrupted, unconditioned being begins to shine. You begin to flower fully as the pure being. You begin to connect with every other being as that spacious ONEness. Let it shine.

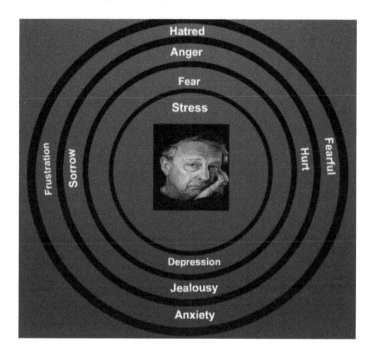

Just to illustrate the power of conditioning, I would like to recount a story.

One morning, a mother returned from the market with a big fish. As usual, she cut the ends off the fish and placed the fish in the oven. Noticing this routine activity, the daughter asked her mother why she had been cutting the ends off the fish before putting it in the oven, to which the mother replied, 'I don't know, I saw my mother do it.' The mother then said, 'Let's go find out from your grandma why she has been cutting the ends off the fish.' The grandmother said, 'I saw my mother do it and I always wanted to ask her. Let's go ask your great grandmother.'

The great grandmother fortunately was alive and the reply from great grandmother was, 'Darling, in those days, the ovens were too small to fit the big fish, so we had to cut the ends to fit the oven.'

Unbeknown to us, we acquire habits which have been passed on from generation to generation. Our likes, dislikes, opinions, beliefs, ideology, anger and fear are all acquired. We may be unaware of it. We may never have questioned this sea of ignorance being passed on from generation to generation—fear, anger, jealousy, hatred, religious belief, ideology, and dogma.

Our brain is cluttered with acquired knowledge from our upbringing and we constantly act and react in relation to this knowledge. Let us call this acquired knowledge 'intellect'. Yes, this knowledge is limited. As a result, everything we do in relation to this limited knowledge will produce a mediocre outcome.

Alternatively, the space between thoughts can be understood as 'unlimited knowing' or 'intelligence'. This space, in which there is no accumulation of past thoughts and no acquired knowledge, can produce the most amazing creativity.

Can you therefore imagine using your brain not as a storehouse for past experiences, but instead as a tool for producing the most creative outcomes in your life? In fact, you are already doing it in emergency situations that call for immediate action. For example, when you see a deadly snake coming towards you, you don't have the time to scan the brain's memory database to determine what action to take. You must respond instantly. At that moment, the thought activity, realising its own limitation, gives way to intelligence, for creative and complete action.

In other words, the limited mind (intellect) surrenders, giving way for the unlimited intelligence to act through you, and like a miracle, it takes you away from the path of the snake to safety.

To summarise, your own brain has all the answers that you need in order to function effectively in this physically manifested world. It is how you make use of your brain that makes the difference. If you visualise your brain as a storehouse for information (from parents, teachers, and society), the 'answers' your brain provides will be limited, second hand, incomplete, and at best, mediocre. Moreover, you will most likely struggle to make things happen in your life.
If, however, you allow the brain to think for itself by questioning the intellect (acquired knowledge), a profoundly beautiful knowing may arise on its own, beyond the realm of the thought and acquired knowledge.

Intellect vs intelligence

Before we proceed further to discussing the pointers that may enable you to access the 'space of peace', it may be beneficial to examine the terms 'intellect' and 'intelligence' as used in this book.

We often hear ourselves say, 'I know' and 'I understand.' Yet what do we really know? And what do we really understand? Where is the knowing coming from? Is not the knowing coming from knowledge that has been acquired from the past? Let us call this 'intellect'. Your 'intellect' consists of a collection of experiences and memories from the past that you have stored in your brain. To 'know' or 'understand' anything, the brain then recollects and draws upon past information and knowledge to provide answers.

Yet the information you have stored may be limited, incomplete, misinformed, and at best outdated. Therefore your 'intellect', which is nothing more than memories (thoughts) of the past stored in your brain, has limited significance in your daily life situation. Yes, we have to acknowledge the fact that some amount of intellect is required to function efficiently in society. For instance, memory is required to get from your house to your place of work or to meet someone at a specified time. To that extent, memory and the 'intellect' is required. However, too much emphasis on the 'intellect'—acquired knowledge—prevents unlimited knowing, what we refer to here as 'intelligence', from arising internally.

To summarise, thoughts make up the limited 'intellect', and the space we referred to earlier can be understood as unlimited 'intelligence'. When there is thought (intellect), there is no space. As a result, there is no space for intelligence to act through you. You struggle.

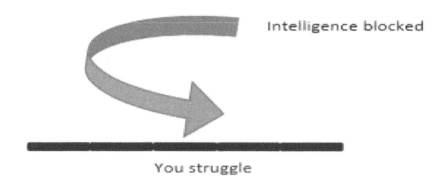

Intelligence blocked

You struggle

When there is no thought, space emerges within you and this space paves the way for intelligence to flow through you. Everything happens for you. Everything aligns itself for you. And there is no more struggle...

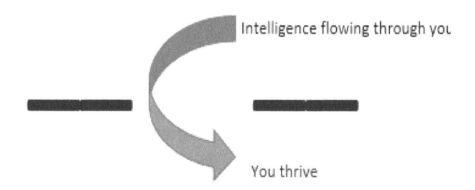

Intelligence flowing through you

You thrive

Intelligence comes into being when the intellect (acquired knowledge) surrenders and says, 'I do not know.' Miracles happen when intelligence prevails. You may recall situations in the past where you have said, 'How did that happen? Where did that come from? I could not have done it—it's a miracle!'. Everything happens for you and you no longer have to struggle to make things happen in life. This is the power of intelligence, which only comes into being when the intellect (thought) surrenders and says, 'I do not know.' In the present moment, for example, when you say you know someone, that person about whom you had prior information (intellect), may have undergone significant changes and may not be the same person you once knew. Most likely however, you are still looking at him or her with preconceived knowledge from the past (intellect)—outdated information you have stored in your memory. The image and the associated knowledge you have of this person is a mental projection from the past and may conflict completely with the current reality. This may then create a barrier between you and the other person, possibly resulting in anger, fear, hatred and stress.

Let me provide an interesting example that you may have observed in your own life. You take some time out of your day-to-day life to spend a few days with your aging parents. However, after only a day or two, you feel a little annoyed because you notice that your parents are looking at you and interacting with you from their mental images, perceptions or experiences from the past. You are not that young child any more. Perhaps you are even interacting with them in relation to preconceived ideas you have of your parents, from when you were younger. This scenario can create much conflict.

Ideally, to reduce or remove the potential for conflict, each party needs to view each other without filters, without preconceived ideas from the past. To do this, it is important to pay attention to the old, limiting thoughts that arise from stored memories and then allow them to dissolve. When this occurs, space is created and you are then able to truly 'see' the other person with clarity and unconditional love.

So, the next time you say, 'I know and I understand,' take a brief moment to pause. If you say, instead, 'I don't know and I don't understand,' you allow knowing to happen. At this time, you are in the present and you are not relying on past, outdated information stored in your memory. Instead, a profound knowing happens in the present moment. You see the other person clearly, in the present moment, not through preconceived mental filters. As a result, any possible barrier between you and the other person dissolves, and love, compassion, understanding, knowing and clarity arise.

We seldom see the true beauty in our surroundings. What we do see is a concept of the object, which is conceived by thoughts from our stored memories. When we look at a flower, for example, our brain is activated and begins to look for information stored in our database of memories. Many thoughts may go through our mind, such as, "Where have I seen this in the past?", "What is the name of the flower?", "Is it similar to other flowers I have seen before?" and, "It would be nice to have this in my garden." These thoughts prevent us from actually "seeing" the true beauty of the flower. Instead, we observe it through filters. The flower is just a beautiful concept.

In order for us to see the real beauty of the flower, we must observe it just as it is in that moment. To do this, there must be space, silence in our head. The constant movement of the mind pendulum must come to a standstill. The mind that wants to classify the flower or name it must be silent. In that silence, in that presence, our brain will not record the image of the flower in our brain cells as memory. Thus, we are able to see the actual beauty of the flower, not just the limited concept of beauty or the mental image of the flower from the past that was stored in our memory bank. To retain this vision, however, we must continue to pay close attention to our thoughts. The instant we become inattentive, the recording will resume, the mind pendulum will begin to move back and forth, our old thoughts will creep in, and the beauty of the flower will be lost.

Your intellect is like a candle flame providing light in a dark room. However, if the intellect envisions itself to be supreme and powerful, it is mistaken. You only need to open the doors and windows and let the natural light of the sun into the room, to see that the power of the candle light is easily diminished. The light of the candle surrenders in the presence of the expansive power of the sun.

Your mind (intellect) considers itself powerful and supreme. You have most likely given it a pedestal to make major life decisions. Indeed, you have been conditioned to position it this way. As a result, you have allowed it to hijack your life. More often than not, you don't even question the decisions that it makes for you. This has serious limitations.

As long as the mind (intellect) considers itself to be supreme and powerful, natural intelligence will be prevented from entering the body. You will thus be operating with the limited intelligence of the mind (intellect or acquired knowledge) and will therefore struggle.

Effectively, only when the mind (intellect) realises its limitations and surrenders can the abundant unlimited natural intelligence begin operating. When this happens, miracles happen and struggle dissipates. Life situations get transformed.

You find that you are now in the lap of unlimited natural intelligence and everything begins happening for you. The experience is one of joy, compassion, love, freedom, peace and total clarity. May I add here, that you cannot force the mind to surrender and become silent? You might like to ask yourself the question: who controls my mind? Is not my own mind controlling itself? If this is the case, trying to control the mind is like running away from the fear of one's own shadow. You cannot win. The mind has to realise its limitations and surrender on its own, thus paving the way for unlimited intelligence to flow through.

How can you do this? Just a simple realisation, observation or awareness that you have been hijacked by the mind is enough for the mind to surrender. Also, you can do it by cultivating less thought and more internal space.

When the unlimited intelligence is allowed to operate within you, miracles happen in your life.

The unlimited intelligence, that pure energy, has the power to cure even the most life- threatening diseases that occur in the human body and which doctors has given up on.
Unlimited potential and possibilities emerge in your life. The right answers, the right actions and the right words come to you. Your body undergoes physical transformation—you know it, and only you

know it. You cannot explain this phenomenon to anyone. You cannot convey it nor teach it to anyone. The moment you try to explain it, it is lost, because you have eluded the unlimited natural intelligence and are back in the limited power of the mind (intellect or incessant thought activity).

Note: The words intellect/thoughts/acquired knowledge/memories all mean the same and denote the conditioned mind.

In summary:

Intellect/thoughts/ mind-full—outcome is mediocre and incomplete

Intelligence/space/ mindful—outcome is creative and complete

No space => Mind-full = > full of thoughts => intellect => selfish => conditioned behaviours like anger, fear and stress reign supreme => actions are mediocre and incomplete and you struggle. Conditional love.

Space => Mindful => no thoughts => intelligence => anger, fear, stress, and all conditioned behaviours have all dissolved at once in this instance => selfless => actions are creative and complete => in this space you experience freedom, joy, beauty, compassion and unconditional love.

Introduction to the pointers

In this current moment, you may be either thinking about something that happened in the past or some events you have planned for future. Our mind is constantly wandering. The pointers are nothing but reminders to bring yourself back to the present moment.

Your mind is like a dog on a leash. The leash is the pointer. The more you allow the dog to wander, the more harm it can cause. The sooner you pull the dog back with the help of the leash, the better for you. The more you notice that your dog is wandering, and the more often you are aware, attentive and try to bring it back, the sooner the dog (on its own) will come to know not to wander any more. Now you don't require the leash any more. Likewise, the more you notice that your mind is wandering away into the PAST or FUTURE, and the more often you try to bring it back the PRESENT, the sooner your mind (on its own) will come to know that it is futile to wander, and the less anxious and stressed you will be in life. In summary, you may require these pointers initially to remind yourself to be in the present, but over a period, with practice, you will no longer require a pointer or reminder to bring yourself back to the present. Being in the present becomes an effortless way of being for you.

There are several pointers that I have used in my life to bring myself back to the present. I will share them in the following chapters. You can choose any of one of these pointers and put it into practice in your daily life. Alternatively, a combination of pointers may help.

But first, a quick analogy to help orient you in your approach to the pointers. Imagine you want to go to New York. There are several ways you can reach New York. You can choose any path. Once you reach New York, you no longer need to know that path. You have reached your destination. Likewise, pointers are paths to get back to your primordial state of being in the present. You can choose any pointer that is comfortable for you to put to practice in your daily life situations, and you can practise it until such time when you no longer require it, to remind you to be in the present. You are always in the present. When you occasionally move back into the past or future, you will be aware of this movement and you can bring yourself back to your primordial present state.

In effect, what you hope to achieve is a situation where you experience more internal pace than previously. Rather than being filled with incessant thought activity, the experience is one of space, and subsequently, the flow of natural intelligence. Space, joy, love and freedom. You are moving back from being unmindful to being mindful.

A note about the role of meditation…

You may have experienced intense peace and stillness when sitting in a quiet room meditating. However, for most of us, this peace is shattered the minute we step out of that quiet room and are confronted with jealousy, anger, fear, and an ego-filled violent society.

My question to you is: if you are unable to bring peace into the whole of your life—whether this be in your chaotic workplace dealing with angry and egoistic workmates, or at home dealing with adolescent children, does the peace that you experience when meditating have limited application in your life? If your answer, like mine, is 'yes', the question then becomes—how can you bring peace into your daily life so that you are able to live in this world free from fear, anger, jealousy, stress and anxiety? How can you exist in modern society as presence, space and peace, when you are surrounded by anger, fear, hatred and violence? How can you exist as a 'space of peace' moment to moment without getting dragged into the madness?

How can you make Life a Meditation rather than your meditation being a 30-minute or one-hour daily affair?

Putting into practice any of the pointers mentioned below will help you become this 'space of peace'. And in the process, you might discover that there is no need to sit in a room and meditate. You can be this 'space of peace' or 'space of creativity' wherever you are—at a busy work place, a board meeting, at home cooking dinner, rushing to pick up your children, arriving late to the office, or even when you are taking a stroll in a park. You can be this moving 'space of peace, space of creativity' wherever you go.

Pointer 1: Observe thoughts, sensations and emotions.

One of the simplest and easiest pointers has already been discussed in this book—observing your thoughts and being attentive or mindful of the precise movement of each thought. In the earlier example of the thought processes surrounding the consumption of an ice cream, this pointer refers to the action of being attentive to the memories of the past experience—for example, the flavour and taste of the ice cream. The minute you become aware of the internal thought process, the thought dissolves. There simply is no thought. And yet in the next moment, a new thought arises, say, for example, the thought of going to see a movie. When you are aware of this new thought, the new thought dissolves and then another thought arises, say, for example, the thought of going out for dinner after the movie. So, this activity involves being mindful of each thought, moment to moment. And noticing how when thoughts dissolve, a brief 'space of peace' emerges, and then a new thought arises to fill this space.

So, the key is to observe and be mindful of the incessant thought activity in your mind. When you observe your thoughts, they dissolve and you experience a brief moment of stillness and peace. Initially, this silence lasts only a short time, but if you endeavour to be very alert and attentive, moment to moment, the time span of space, silence or peace will increase. Eventually, the length of time you are able to be alert and attentive will be sufficient enough to pave the way for the experience of abundant space in your life.

Similarly, you can practise observing sensations and feelings. Are anger, fear, anxiety and stress part of your being? You may believe so. You live and die with them, don't you? Yet, you are not born with these experiences. Therefore, these are your conditioned behaviours (anger, fear and so forth) that you must have acquired sometime during your upbringing. If so, can we not put an end to those conditioned behaviours? How can you put an end to them?

Through observation… by being mindful of the fear, the jealousy, the rage, the feeling of betrayal. When you are attentive (mindful) to these emotions arising, the emotions subside. If you are not attentive (unmindful), you give the emotions the space to over-power and act through you, causing you to become more and more anxious and stressed. Or, realising you have been fearful or angry or jealous later on, generally leaves you with a feeling of regret—'I shouldn't have been angry…I shouldn't have been jealous.' This type of thinking is truly detrimental to your overall wellbeing.

So the aim is to notice, be mindful, for example, when fear arises —'look, there it is, fear.' You are attentive (aware or mindful) to the fear and then the fear passes. It may come back again, but the key is to remain vigilant, attentive and mindful, moment to moment. You become awareness, more mindful that these conditioned behaviours do not act through you—or rather, that you do not give them the power that they are seeking. You are that awareness in which the fear is arising and subsiding, and you are not identifying with it and giving it energy to overpower and hurt you or anyone else.

This constant observation and awareness or mindfulness of thoughts and feelings, as and when they arise in you, whether you are at work with your colleagues or at home with your loved ones, is the secret to fulfilling a peaceful and struggle-free life. It is a simple equation to end your suffering and live a life free from anger, fear, stress, ego, anxiety, hatred, jealousy and violence. It is also the way out of ignorance. A state in which you are able to fully forgive. Forgive others for their ignorance. For being unmindful and allowing the conditioned behaviours to overtake them and be expressed through them. Now that you are more mindful, you are at peace with yourself and therefore you are able to forgive others when they are angry with you. Only when you are in the present, when you are that space of peace, can you really forgive someone.

As many enlightened beings have stated over the centuries in various ways—'Please forgive them. They are ignorant and they know not what they are doing.'

When you pay attention, in other words, when you are mindful, thought activity is disrupted and your mind does not have to continually struggle to concentrate and resist the temptation of distraction. Your brain is fresh and rejuvenated, with plenty of energy available for creative action in your life. Paying attention—being mindful—creates silence and space, which makes room for joy, love, compassion, intelligence, creativity, wholeness, goodness and oneness. This is 'living in the moment.' Is this not what we strive for? Is it not our goal to live in the present with full awareness?

The key to maintaining full attention is observation. You must be constantly mindful of your thought taking you away from this present moment into the past or to the fantasy world of the future. When you are, you are constantly in the present moment and therefore free of all the past baggage of conditioned behaviours.

Remember thought gives rise to your conditioned behaviours. When there are no thoughts, you are free of all the conditioned behaviours like anger, fear, anxiety, stress and so on…Freedom.

How can we put this to practice?

Observing your thoughts is something that we are not used to doing and therefore it may be a bit difficult to practice initially. If so, you can start practising it progressively. Allocate 10 minutes in the morning and 10 minutes before going to bed. Sit comfortably on a chair, relax your body and gently close your eyes. Now effortlessly observe the thoughts arising and disappearing in your head. Just notice the thoughts. Ah, there it is… another thought… another one and so on…

As you practice with the 4Ds, you will slowly begin to notice an increase in the time of awareness; from 10 minutes to 20 and 30 and so on, depending upon your practice.

After a few months of practice, you can now do the same with your eyes open. The challenge with keeping your eyes open is that there are several things in the room and your mind begins to judge these objects, taking you aware from being in the present. Therefore, be mindful. With practise, you can observe the thoughts arising and subsiding. If your mind is judging, observe that judgement. Notice any emotions arising in you. You may be feeling restless, feeling bored, observe that. When you are mindful and observe these thoughts and emotions very attentively you will not allow these emotions or thoughts to overpower you or act through you. You are now the master. The thoughts and emotions the slave. If you are unmindful you give the thoughts and emotions the power to act through you. Therefore, be a mindful observer moment to moment.

After several months of practice, first with your eyes closed, and then with your eyes open, you may then be able to take this practice wherever you go and to whatever you are doing. Just observe the thoughts and emotions when you are walking towards the office, at home when you are doing your cooking or doing other chores. Just observe any thoughts which may be taking you away into the past or future. The moment you notice that your mind is wandering, you have directed yourself back to the PRESENT. Therefore, constantly remind yourself to observe your thoughts. At first you may find this difficult. However, with practice (Practice with 4D's) this will become second nature. It will. Because being in the PRESENT is our primordial nature. Therefore practice, practice and practice until you no longer require any pointers or reminders. Now, you are always in the Present however when you move away into the past or future you will notice it, you will be aware it. The moment you notice it you are back in the Present.

Inattention or Being Unmindful =>You are allowing the thought to dominate, which creates 'the self', or rather, the limited 'false self', an identity of who you are with your name and baggage like fear, anger, ego => this creates disorder, conflict, anxiety frustration and a mediocre life.

Attention or Being Mindful => No thought movement => The 'self' with its baggage like fear, anger, ego is dissolved => This gives rise to joy, awareness, compassion, love and creativity in life.

To keep it simple:

Imagine your thoughts and emotions to be a poisonous snake ready to strike. When you are inattentive (unmindful), the snake will strike and inject the poison of fear, anger, anxiety, and stress and so on. On the other hand, when you are attentive, (mindful) the snake will stay away from you. Can you be mindful moment to moment? This will require practice. This will require some effort.

However, with constant practice, being mindful will come naturally to you as this is your primordial state. You once had that mindfulness as a child. You have moved away. Now you are getting back to your primordial state of being mindful, aware, totally present and free of all that conditioning.

Inattention or being unmindful = Paving the way for thoughts, which gives rise to disorder, conflict, anger, fear, hatred and thus a mediocre life.

Attention or being mindful = No thoughts—space, peace, order, awareness, joy, compassion, love, freedom and thus a life filled with creativity.

Pointer 2: Ask yourself, 'What am I thinking?'.

Another simple practice is to ask yourself, 'what am I thinking?'. The moment you ask the question, you become mindful of your thought activity and there are no more thoughts. You have come back to the present. Just space and silence. In other words, the moment you become aware (mindful) that you are thinking (whether about a past or future event), you come into the present moment and regain the space, the lost space. The space that is always there, just usually obscured by thoughts.

Ask yourself what I am I thinking now? This question brings you back from whatever you are thinking, either about the past or the future, back to the present moment. How often can you remind yourself to ask this question in a day? Initially, it may be just a few times. With practice, you may be able to do so several times and then with even more practice, you do not need to ask this question at all. You are always in the present moment. Because you are mindful, you will catch yourself moving back into the thought-dominated world of past or future.

If you are feeling angry, upset, stressed, lonely, anxious or fearful, know that you have moved away from being in the present moment. Bring yourself back quickly to the primordial state of being in the present. In the present, everything is as good as it can be. There is no longer the worries of the past or the anxiety of the future. Get rooted in this moment. Be mindful. Remember thoughts give rise to your conditioned behaviours like anger, fear, anxiety, stress, loneliness and so on. When you are mindful, there are no thoughts, you are not thinking anymore, you are in the present, free from the past baggage of conditioned behaviours.

Pointer 3: Ask yourself, 'Am I in the present?'.

The moment you ask yourself, 'am I in the present?', you become present. Your thoughts, as previously mentioned, generally take you either to the past or the future. It is very rare for them to be connected to the present moment. However, the moment you ask this question, your thoughts dissolve, you find yourself anchored to the present moment and 'space' becomes available to you. When you find that you slip back into thinking (and thus, into the past or future), you can ask yourself again, 'am I in the present?'.

This may be a challenging practice in your day-to-day life because you may be so used to thoughts taking you into the past or the future. This has been your default. You have been conditioned since childhood to be in thought mode. And yet now, you are being asked to reverse this tendency and make space and awareness the default mode. This is like kicking a habit. We know cigarette smoking is not good for our health, yet it is difficult to give up smoking. We know that exercise is good for the body, yet we don't take the time to exercise every day. Yet if you can get a glimpse of the space and freedom available to you by following these pointers, I am confident that you will not want to go back to same struggle and stressful life. Initially, you may find that a great deal of effort and energy is required to practise. However, like the ignition of a car, once it catches fire and the momentum picks up, very little energy is required to be in the state of presence or space. In other words, being that space is effortless. This is in fact our primordial state and therefore requires no effort. When you experience even a small amount of effort in trying to be that space know that you have moved away from being that space.

In that space of awareness (mindfulness), thoughts, feelings and sensations that are nothing but the conditioned behaviours or habits acquired during your upbringing will simply arise and pass away. You no longer act and react to those thoughts and feelings as you did previously. Rather, you will become awareness, or become mindful. You are awareness. Awareness is aware of fear, anger and various other emotions arising in you. You do not, however, give it the power to act through you. Let it come and let it pass. Just as the clouds come and go in the vast sky, thoughts, feelings and sensations will simply arise and pass away. The clouds do not and cannot overwhelm the vast sky, and neither should your thoughts, feelings and sensations overwhelm you. Awareness of fear dissolves fear, awareness of anger dissolves anger. Likewise, awareness of any emotion dissolves that emotion. The difference is previously you were unaware of the emotions overpowering you. You are now fully aware of these emotions and therefore they don't overpower you and react through you anymore. Effectively, an altogether new world emerges, a world of peace and freedom. A world that has always been there for you, but one that generally becomes obscured by the mechanisms of the mind.

Please note that the word 'awareness' can conjure up a lot of meaning. I am not referring to the intellectual understanding or understanding by the mind. When that mind noise ceases, in that silence there is an awareness. By 'awareness' I mean your entire being, all the 10 trillion cells become fully alert, your sense perception comes alive, attentive and therefore totally aware. This is beyond words but when it happens in you, you will know it and you will feel it in your entire being. This is the 'awareness' I am attempting to point to in this book.

Pointer 4: Observe vast space.

Have you ever looked up at the sky and noticed migratory birds flying towards their destination after sun set? Or noticed birds resting on a roof top? On a dark night, have you noticed the sky dotted with innumerable stars? Or various cloud formations with the sun slowly setting on the horizon?

Birds, stars, clouds…everything in the cosmos is arranged neatly in order, with 'perfect space' between them. Coming back to earth, trees and flowers need space between them in order to grow and flourish. Are you aware of this space? As children, we are conditioned to notice 'things' and ignore the space. In fact, the vastness of space is obscured by the 'things' around us.

As mentioned earlier, as children, we are fascinated with toys; we want more and more toys. Growing up, we start to accumulate more toys, bigger toys—the newest iPhone, the latest model car, a house or houses, top brand clothing and shoes. Yet in the process of this accumulation, we also become acquainted with anger, fear, stress, hatred, jealousy and so forth. We lose sense of space and instead become all-consumed with our possessions, thoughts and feelings.

Different forms of life—humans, plants, micro-organisms—originate, thrive and perish in this space. The sun rises from and disappears into this space. Wind arises and passes away, the rain also casts its spell and vanishes into the space. Birth and death happen constantly in this space. And the space just observes these shapes or various forms coming and going, ever watchful, remaining steady, eternal, immortal.

This fourth pointer asks you to become reacquainted with space—the space around you, as well as the space within. It invites you to listen to space. To become absorbed in space. To become familiar with its quietness…its peace. Noise will continue arising and passing away —thoughts and feelings too—but with this practice, your attention is on vast space. Staying connected to, and present with, vast space.

The next time you are out walking in a garden, take a moment to observe the space around you in which there may be trees, grass, flowers, birds, the sky and insects flying around. Enjoy the feeling of space…enjoy noticing space…

And at night, when you are lying in bed and several thoughts come into your head concerning the past (things that happened during the day) and the future (what am I doing tomorrow?), turn your attention to the vast space around you, the space above, the space to your sides, and the space below you. In this way, the incessant thought activity will dissolve and you will find yourself back in the present moment. Unlike things in this space, this emptiness cannot be judged. There is no movement of thought when you observe this space. No mental projections. You are no longer looking through the filters of the conditioned mind, therefore there is no barrier between you and the other being. Just a oneness, a sense of being one with everything.

In other words, incessant thought activity (intellect) comes to a standstill for the first time, allowing actual observation to happen. Allowing 'intelligence' (knowing) to flow through you. Clarity.

Beauty. A sense of oneness. The knowing that you are no longer a separate entity. Rather, you are one with vast space. You are space. This is a new way of living.

This 'way of living' is very difficult for our minds to comprehend. This is not within the reach of the 'normal conditioned' mind. Yet the workings of the 'normal' mind (incessant thought activity, or the intellect) are precisely what prevents us from recognising that we are that vast space. So let us learn how to slow down the incessant movement of our mind pendulum and ultimately allow it to come to a standstill (present) allowing the unlimited knowing (intelligence) to arise. This knowing knows that space is eternal, does not die, and is everlasting. All manifested 'things', including your body, will perish, while that space is indestructible. You are that space. The only thing that is preventing you from knowing that you are that eternal space is your own incessant mind activity or the constant movement of your mind pendulum.

When you observe the vast space around you, the mind activity comes to a standstill and you are in the present. In other words, when the mind activity comes to a standstill, when there is no more thought activity, this space of no thoughts within will recognise this space without (on the outside). When there is no space within and you are consumed or hijacked by thoughts, you tend to miss that space within and the space outside. Your life is consumed by thing after thing or thought after thought. The space is gone, missing from our lives, and thus we suffer.

When we are identified with space, we are able to witness our bodies moving, growing and dying. We no longer identify with our body and the baggage associated with it. We are not attached to our body and its baggage. When you are no longer attached, there is no longer the fear. There is freedom from all fears, including the fear of death. You are eternal. You are that space, you are indestructible. Your body may live as long as you give it a good environment to live. Like everything, your body has a finite life and then perishes. You are not that body. You are that space in which the body and other forms come and go. You are that manifested consciousness, awareness, mindfulness, nothingness, higher energy or simply the space, which is eternal. This is not a spiritual or philosophical fantasy. We simply know this when the mind activity comes to a halt.

No need to believe me or anyone else for that matter. Inquire and discover this for yourself. You are eternal. You are space.

Pointer 5: Observe the breath.

We breathe, yet we are mostly unaware or unmindful this is happening. We humans have destined it to a mechanical action that happens continuously and as a result, we take it for granted.

However, if you notice your breath—if you become aware or mindful that you are breathing in and breathing out—you may discover that there is no room for thoughts. Instead, space opens up, allowing 'intelligence' to flow through. Space becomes available because you are resting solidly in the present, aware or mindful of each breath, moment to moment.
The moment this attention waivers, the moment you are unmindful, you allow thoughts to enter, taking you back into the past or forward into the future, meaning the space is lost. You are no longer in the present moment.

Notice or observe and be mindful about your own breathing as a way of bringing you to a place of silence, of no thoughts. Also, notice that every time you breathe in, you are taking in air from vast space, and when you breathe out, you are breathing out into that vast empty space. The space of creativity, the space of intelligence.

Pointer 6: Perceive your senses.

In your frantic dash to get from one place to another, have you ever paused for a moment to listen to the sound of a train passing by in the distance? Do try it sometime. The sound is captivating.

When you are listening intently to the sound of the train passing by, your mind chatter comes to an abrupt halt in that moment. You are in the present. You listen fully... You enjoy the sound. You are now using your sense perception to bring you from the past or the future into the present. Above all, you listen with clarity, without the accompanying incessant mind chatter.

Alternatively, the next time you are in a park or garden, use your sense of hearing to listen to the birds singing, the sound of the breeze, the creaking noise of the wind in the trees, or the noise insects make to attract their mates. You can also use your sense of smell to inhale the beautiful fragrance of flowers in the air or smell freshly mown grass.

When you are sitting in a coffee shop and enjoying a coffee, just smell the coffee, feel the taste of the coffee in your mouth. Don't take it for granted. Be a bit more mindful and notice that beautiful flower, the love heart or any other artwork that the barista makes with milk with so much love and attention in your cup of coffee. By being mindful of all that you are in the present, moment to moment, you will notice everything, you will listen, you will have come alive because you are mindful, and thoughts have not hijacked you into the past or future.

When you are listening, watching and smelling, your mind is quiet. In that moment there are no thoughts. You are in the present. The moment there are no thoughts you experience space, silence, peace or presence. The space within recognize the space without (or on the outside). In that space of silence your sense perceptions are very alert, alive and working fully. You begin to listen to even the minutest of noise which you would not have picked had you been thinking about the past or future. When you are that space of silence you include everything and exclude nothing. You can listen, you can smell and you can see everything simultaneously all happening in that space. You are not excluding anything. You can listen, feel and see everything that is happening within you and on the outside, simultaneously. Within you, you can feel your heart beating, you can feel the tummy murmur, you can observe the thoughts coming and going, you are fully aware of your breathing in breathing out, and on the outside, you will notice and feel the gentle breeze, the flowers dancing in the breeze, the butterflies flying around, the trees swaying away in the wind, the bark of the trees peeling away, the ants gathering food, the sound of the train passing and finally fading, the birds singing and making merry on top of the tree, the beauty of the rose in the garden and even the fresh natural wax on the blade of a newly sprouted grass and many more. All happening simultaneously in that space and you are just observing and not judging. You have come alive. You begin to notice the beauty all around. This is true living, truly one with nature and all others forms in that space. This to me is Meditation, if you want to call it that way.

The moment you become unmindful/unaware/inattentive, you allow thoughts to come in, you become anxious again. You start reviewing the past and anticipating the future. You move out of the present moment. You have come back to the old mechanical or Mediocre way of living.

So be alert, attentive and mindful for any thought movement in your head. Even if a thought comes into your head, just say, 'look another thought!' This will bring you back into the present. Simple, isn't it?

Pointer 7: Be aware or mindful of every action in your daily life.

We are mostly unmindful of everything that we do in life, aren't we? We wake up in the morning and go straight to the bathroom to brush our teeth. When we are brushing our teeth, we are thinking of taking a shower. When we are in the shower, we are thinking about breakfast. When we are having our breakfast, we are thinking about the peak hour traffic on the road. When we are stuck in the traffic, we are thinking of being late for the meeting. When we are in the meeting, we are thinking about our lunch. When we are having lunch, we are thinking about the meeting scheduled for the afternoon. When we are at the meeting, we are thinking about picking up the children. When we are picking up the children, we are thinking about dinner tonight. When we are cooking dinner, we are thinking about the meeting for tomorrow. Can you the see this vicious cycle?

Generally speaking, we are most often unaware of everything we do in our daily lives. Are our actions so mechanical, unmindful or mediocre? Have we simply reduced our actions to an act or means to an end? I will leave this with you to ponder...

Being totally aware of, mindful of and attentive to all of your actions in daily life—for example, brushing your teeth, drinking a bottle of water, looking at yourself in the mirror, tying your shoe laces, picking up a cup of coffee, can all take you to that space of peace and presence. Even boring mundane chores can become really interesting when you are fully aware and when you don't make the activity a 'means to an end'.

Let's imagine for a moment that you are a bit late for a meeting. You are running to get there on time. Usually, you are unmindful that you are running, as your mind is preoccupied with the agenda for the meeting, and a lot of questions may be coming up in your mind about the meeting. These might be questions like, for example, am I going to disappoint my managers today? I am going to feel miserable for being late? Have I prepared well for the meeting? Have I got my presentation in order? So many thoughts, aren't there? Mostly thinking about the future event. Just enough to make you nervous and anxious.

Can you be mindful or aware that you are running or walking fast? If so, you have brought yourself back to the present moment. You are not thinking so much about the meeting at the present moment. You are just walking or running. You are mindful or fully aware that you are running or walking fast. You are not reducing that activity of running or walking fast to a mere mechanical action or stepping stone to the next moment. You begin to enjoy the journey. You are not so anxious because you are not thinking about the future event, the meeting. You are comfortably in the present.

Imagine now that you are observing a flower. You can observe it just mechanically, unmindfully. When you do so, what you see is the mental image of the flower that you have conceived in your mind. The peripheral beauty.

Alternatively, when you are AWARE you are observing a flower, that which you are observing undergoes a transformation. Not really. It's the same flower which was always there. You are just now more mindful. You are able to observe this flower and the beauty of it as new and not something conceived by the mind.

When you are mindful, you begin to see the beauty not only in flowers but in everything that you see around you. This is being aware and mindful of everything that you are doing. But don't take my word for it—just realise this for yourself and notice the difference it brings in your own life. Be fully there, totally rooted in each particular activity, and you will be in the present.

Pointer 8 : Focus your attention on your body.

When you find it difficult to go to sleep at night, try to focus your attention on your body. Bring yourself back from wandering off to thinking about those past events you had at work or being anxious thinking about the future events that you have lined up for tomorrow by focusing your attention on your body. As you lie in your bed, start with your toes. Put your full attention on your toes, and then your legs and slowly move back up your legs to your stomach, your chest, your heart, your neck, and your head. Now go back from your head all the way to your toes. Try doing this 2 or 3 times, and before you know it, you would have fallen asleep. By focusing your attention on your body, you bring yourself back to the present moment.

Pointer 9 : Surrender to this moment.

For the mind, this moment is boring. It's always looking forward to the next moment, the future. Is there an end to it? Is not the future something that is conceived by your own mind? There is only this moment. NOW, this moment. Everything is perfect and in order in this moment. Surrender to it fully. Dwell in this moment. If you resist this moment, you will struggle. When you accept this moment, you will go beyond it and something profound comes into being.

Take a gentle stroll in your local garden. You will notice the perfect synchrony and harmony with which nature aligns itself. The rocks on your path are lying still where they should be, the dead leaves that have departed from their branches a long while ago are lying perfectly where they should be and the flowers are neatly lined along the foot path in various colours and sizes where they should be. The outer layers of bark are just trying to peel off from the trunk of a tree as they should be, the branches of the trees are dancing to the tune of the gentle early morning breeze, the lonely bird is singing and even the early morning drizzle—there perhaps to quench the thirst of the plants—and the thorny bushes in the garden, are all perfectly aligned and beautifully synchronized.

It's only our mind that says, if it had been this way, it would have been nice and beautiful. Or, if only it was not drizzling, it would have been nice. If it was not as windy, it would have been nice. And so on. Beyond the mind, everything is as it should be...

perfectly in order. Surrender to this moment. Just be in this moment. Do not resist what is happening now in this moment. You will begin to experience beauty, joy and freedom moment to moment when you surrender to this moment.

Pointer 10 : How can I BE that space of peace, moment to moment?

The moment you wake up in the morning, you experience a state of 'not knowing' anything. It's a beautiful feeling in which you don't remember anything of the past nor of the future, a state of complete presence. Unfortunately, you will be in that state for only a brief moment before your mind will kick in and quickly entice you to ponder if it's a Monday, or Tuesday or Wednesday? Followed by a feeling of 'oh no!'. When the mind has figured out what day it is, it will also remind you of the various activities lined up for the day and into the evening. This is enough to create anxiety in you while you are still lying in bed.

How would you like to prolong that beautiful state of 'not knowing'; a state of presence in which you are not thinking about the past or the future—just lying awake in your bed in the morning?

This can be achieved by combining all of the above pointers.

You can start by simply looking at the empty space around you in the room. When you look at the space around you, there are no thoughts in your head. Just space. You may listen to the sound of the birds singing early in the morning, thus utilising sense perception. Then you might slowly rise from your bed and place your legs in that space. Be fully aware that you are getting out of your bed and going into the bathroom. Be aware that you are reaching for the toothbrush and applying toothpaste to the brush.

Normally you may not be aware of these actions and activities because you may be thinking about the tasks and meetings lined up for your day. As a result, these activities may be reduced to mechanical actions performed automatically with little conscious awareness. You may be reducing these actions to a means to the next action and the next and so on...

You might now step into the shower and be aware of the water falling on to your body. Be aware of the soap and its texture. Be aware of the shampoo and feel it in your hair. Thoughts about the peak hour traffic or meetings you may be attending that day will certainly come into your head. Just observe them. The moment you observe them, you are back in the present.

When you are driving your car in traffic, just observe the thoughts that arise. Observe the traffic lights, the colours, the birds swooping and flying, other cars moving past. Notice these things. They are all happening in vast space. The fewer thoughts we have, the more we will be able to experience vast space internally and externally. This 'space' will assist us to see blades of grass on the side of the road with clarity. Small flowers showing off their beauty, saying to you, 'look I have bloomed for you. Have a beautiful day.'

Be aware of your breath and again observe the thoughts coming into your head. If required, ask yourself, 'what am I thinking?' Or, 'am I in the present?'. When you are in a meeting, you can observe the space around your colleagues and look at them with 'fresh eyes', devoid of judgements, past stories and preconceived ideas. In this way, 'barriers' between them and you may be reduced, and your colleagues may be inspired to interact and connect with you at a deeper level. Furthermore, positive outcomes may start to be reached with ease and your colleagues may even want to begin hanging out with you.

In essence, all of the pointers in this book will help steer you back into the present.

If you want to reach a meeting venue at a certain time and you are running late, you can walk fast or run to make up time—but the main thing is to be *aware or mindful* that you are running or walking fast. Any action that is performed with awareness or mindfulness will take you to that space of peace, space of presence.

Similarly, you may be packing your bag in a hurry and running late to catch a flight. You may choose to reduce the packing to a mechanical action, a means to the next action, thus provoking anxiety and possibly causing you to miss a few items that are required for the journey, or you may breathe calmly and act with total awareness, thus allowing intelligence to flow through you. This, in turn, will enable you to pack the necessary items and catch your flight on time. You allow the intellect (thoughts) to step aside so that intelligence can act through you causing everything to 'miraculously' align along the way. When you are in the process of typing on your keyboard, notice the vast space on your computer screen, notice the keyboard, be aware of the action of your fingers typing, the words flowing through you easily as well as words that seem to appear magically on the screen—words that you have never heard of before—and yet, capture what you wish to say perfectly and meaningfully in that moment.

You may wonder—did I write that? The answer is—yes. You are simply in the present, free from incessant thought activity, and therefore you have allowed intelligence to act through you.

When you are reading this book now in this moment, notice the space around each word. The moment you notice that space, the words stand out with clarity. I have intentionally provided space between each word/s in this book. Notice that space between the words. You are now in the present, devoid of any thought activity.

Allow intelligence to work for you and see the miracles occur in your life. Intelligence can only flow through you unobstructed if you have space within, when you are in the present, when there are no thoughts in your head, or when you are aware or mindful of the thought activity in your head.

Plants, birds, animals and the whole of nature is united and lives in harmony. They thrive together. The intelligence or higher energy is flowing through them, unhindered. There is a feeling of **ONEness** amongst these forms. It's only us humans who characterise ourselves as separate and disconnect ourselves from the natural world. This is because of the incessant thought activity which overwhelms us. A bird sitting on the branch of a tree does not think– 'Should I fly to next branch? Will I fall?' It just moves instinctively, never hindered by thoughts. Likewise, a seed sprouts, becomes a plant and grows into a mighty tree. Everything just happens. It's only us human forms who struggle in life, because of our incessant thought activity which is preventing the intelligence to act through us. Let us learn from the nature around us. Let us learn to witness and experience the miracle of life, just as the other life forms on earth thrive.

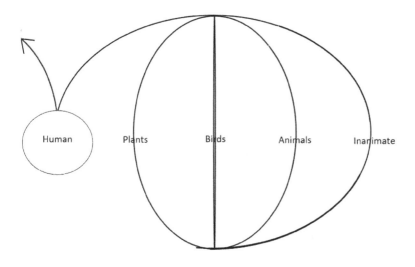

The dark layers around the human forms in the above picture is the incessant thought activity which prevents the intelligence from flowing freely. Intelligence or higher energy is unhindered for plants, animals, birds and all other forms except for humans.

Allow intelligence to work for you and see the miracles occur in your life. Intelligence can only flow through you unobstructed if you have **space** within, when you are in the present, when there are no thoughts in your head, or when you are aware or mindful of the thought activity in your head.

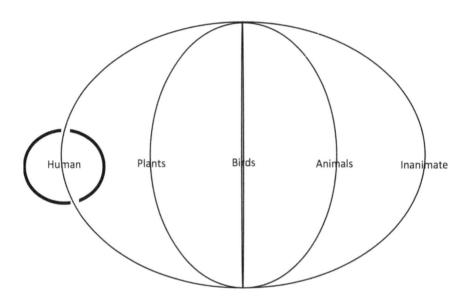

ONEness – One with every other form

When you go for a stroll through a garden, observe the vast space in the garden, complete with trees, plants, flowers, and butterflies happily flying around. Notice the slight breeze, the vast sky in which the clouds come and go. Listen to the birds singing, smell the fragrance of the flowers in the air, observe the thoughts in your head, look at the grass lined up on both sides of the walking track, notice the dew sticking on the blades of the grass, the amazing display of colour when the rays of the sun kiss the dew.

Acknowledge that you are able to see these things with clarity because you have space in your head—incessant thought activity has dissipated. Everything looks so beautiful, everything is as it should be, the space within recognises the space without, and you experience yourself as one with everything. When you are one with everything, how can you even imagine hurting anything? If you do hurt someone or something, are you not in fact hurting yourself? You *ARE* that space in which everything comes and goes. The plants, the trees, the animals and humans, all come and go in this space. Your body is born, it develops and then perishes in this space. Animate and inanimate things arise and pass away in this space. Your body will last as long as you provide it with a stress-free environment and nutritious food. Then, like every organism, it will perish. But you are not the body. You are this space. You *ARE* this space that never dies. You are eternal. The only thing that is preventing you from recognising this are the thoughts in your head.

Be this awareness, witnessing everything around you moment to moment and notice that everything aligns itself for you like a miracle. There is so much beauty, compassion, joy and benevolence all around you wherever you go. You are this oneness. One with everything—ants, plants, animals, humans, the whole of the cosmos.

You have moved back from mind-full to being mindful. You have come back home where you effortlessly belong. In the present moment, where there is a lot of space. Space of peace or space of no thoughts. You are this space, or spaciousness, in which everything happens. You are eternal.

Epilogue

Now it is time to part ways. Now it is time for you to put the pointers I have put forward in this book into practice in your daily life. Each of these pointers or reminders will assist you to have some respite from incessant thought activity and reconnect with the much-needed space inside of you—the space of creativity.

Buddha, Jesus, Ramana Maharishi, Mohammed, J.Krishnamurti —and many others who have remained inconspicuous—all realised one thing that changed their lives... They realised that they should not give much importance to their thoughts.
They realised the natural state of human beings. They realised the space within and without.

This space is possible for you now in this moment. However, what you have just read in this book will remain on the level of concepts and words unless you put the pointers into practice in your life.

After reading this book, you may find several questions arising in your mind. If so, please ask yourself if the questions are coming from the level of your intellect (conditioned mind, or incessant thought activity) or if you are connected to intelligence and vast space.

If you still require an answer to your question, I would ask you to delve deep within to discover the answer. Place the question in the vast space of your mind where there is no thought movement. In that space of silence, all answers will reveal themselves to you at the right time. A profound knowing (answer) will arise... coming from the place of unlimited intelligence. Once you can access this intelligence, you no longer need to depend on anyone else to answer your questions or to assist you on your life's journey. You are in the lap of the unlimited.

Just as an example, I have used the concepts in this book to answer below a few questions that have come up before in my mind. These answers did not come from the limited intellect. I allowed unlimited intelligence to provide me with the answers— in that silence when there was no thought activity.

How do I know if I am on the right path?

If those circumstances or situations that made you angry, anxious, fearful, and stressed no longer make you so, you are on the right path. In other words, anger, anxiety, fear and stress will continue to exist in society. But you have changed. You are mindful, aware and conscious, and therefore you have dissolved your past baggage. You are now looking at the world without those glasses of conditioning. You are that space of peace. You are able to forgive. You are able to accept. You will now not be dragged into that madness. Your body and all the 10 trillion cells that make up all the organs are thriving, and this will show up in your whole being. You will feel that newfound sense of clarity, peace, freedom creativity and joy in you. Be that moving space of peace wherever you are and whatever you do. You will notice this change in you and others around you will notice it as well.

Here are some benchmarks:

* When your spouse has said something unpleasant about you, you don't react (previously you acted or reacted by defending or arguing).

* When you are driving and someone from behind is honking, overtaking you and looks at you with disgust, you don't react... you allow them to pass.

* When you missed your bus or train this morning, you don't feel anxious as you usually do but rather tell yourself, "it's OK. I'll take the next one...".

* When you are waiting for your friend at a coffee shop, and he or she doesn't turn up, you don't feel impatient as you usually do.

* When you accidentally meet someone who has caused a lot of harm or grief in your life, yet you are able to forgive him or her....

(Be aware that all these are possible ONLY in that "space of presence" or in that space of no thoughts.)

In other words, the things or circumstances that previously made you angry, anxious, fearful, stressed, impatient and so on, no longer make you so. You no longer act or react, but just accept. You have now begun the journey.

Does it take time for me to realise that space of peace? Does it take time for me to become mindful?

Being mindful is your primordial state. As a child you were very mindful, aware and attentive. You have moved away from that innateness. Moving back to being mindful can only happen now, in this moment. What does that mean? It has taken several years for us to be in the state of being unmindful that we are. A state of constant and compulsive thinking. Thinking about the past or future. This has been our habit for the past several years. Now we need to kick that habit. How?

The moment you observe that you are thinking, you are back in the present. In other words, just being mindful that you are thinking means you're in the present. Does this take time? Well, it can happen right now, in this instance, can it not? However, because of our habit, we usually move back into our habit of several years, which is the habit of thinking. So, be mindful again. You are now in the present. With constant reminders, you can bring yourself back from the past or future back to the present.

This may require some discipline and effort initially. Over a period of time, being rooted in the present becomes our habit. We have moved from being unmindful to being mindful, which is our primordial state. Being in our primordial state now requires no more effort. Effortlessly at peace with ourselves. It can happen in this instant—in the moment you are mindful that you are thinking.

In essence, the pointers that I have presented here provide a pathway or ladder to a space of peace and to accessing unlimited intelligence or profound knowing. As mentioned though, after a period, you may find that you no longer need to practise these pointers. Instead, you may find an underlying awareness remains within you and you are simply aware when you drift into thoughts. In other words, you become awareness itself, aware of thoughts coming and going, and you no longer require the pointers. When this happens, you will know it. You will feel it in your physical being. At this point, unlimited intelligence will be flowing through you at all times.

This is important—we do not want to keep practising the pointers ad infinitum. Sometimes we can get stuck at the level of the pointers, analysing this pointer and that pointer and never getting anywhere. At some point, the pointers must be dissolved. In other words, the ladder must be withdrawn so that you can reach home, the spaciousness that you are—space within and space without. Anger, sadness, happiness, fear, anxiety, stress and all other emotions will continue to exist in this physically manifested world, but when you are that space, or when you are mindfully in the present, emotions like anger, fear, anxiety and stress don't affect you anymore. Like the clouds in the sky, let them come and let them go.

You are that awareness or mindfulness and therefore you will catch those emotions before they overpower you and act through you. Previously, you were unaware and therefore you allowed the emotions to overpower you and act through you.

In real-life situations when these emotions no longer affect you—when you get a feeling that you are no longer dragged into that madness—you have begun to free yourself from everything. Space, presence, peace, joy, (unconditional) love and freedom open up for you. When this happens, you will know it in your physical being.

To conclude, I encourage you to take the time to delve deep into your life. I encourage you to question the way you have been living, question the way you have been using your own brain and understand the conditioning you have received. Books and teachers may provide some guidance, but ultimately it is up to you to shine your own light. Only you can be this space. The space *between thoughts which I call intelligence.*

Final important points to be aware of:

1. Your thoughts give rise to your conditioning—your past baggage.

2. When you observe your thoughts, the thought activity dies or is dissolved.

3. It is not the thought that is the problem. It is being unmindful that is the problem. If you are mindful, you will be aware of the thought hijacking you into the past or future. You are mindful. You now have the power. You have not given away that power to thoughts. You are the master and the thoughts the slave.

4. We humans have the power to use the intellect as and when required for our day to day functioning in the society and to keep it at bay when not required. The power to switch between intellect and intelligence. Do not give away that power to the limited intellect, which is your mind. If you do so you will struggle. When the intellect is kept at bay the intelligence prevail. May that intelligence prevail in every being.

For those of you who are able to better grasp with pictures I have used my own left, right hand and the fingers to summarize our self - discovery.

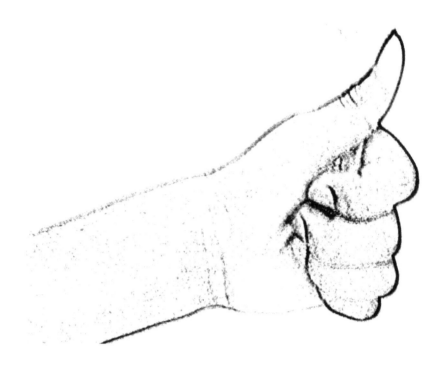

FREEDOM, JOY, LOVE, SELF LESS & COMPASSION

Imagine your left arm with fingers folded (as above in this picture) to be the pure unconditioned true being, like you were when you were a child. It is new, uncorrupted and experiences absolute joy.

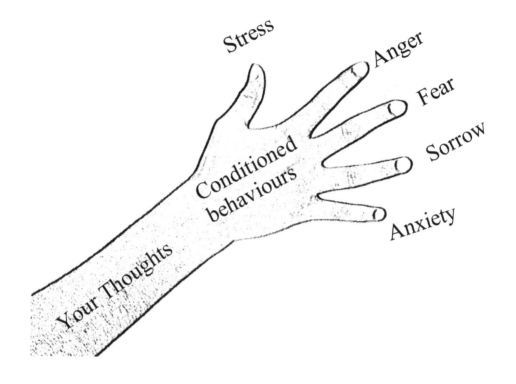

Now, imagine your right hand as your thoughts, and the fingers as your conditioned behaviours or all the conditioning that you have acquired during your life. The thoughts give rise to your conditioning or conditioned behaviours, resulting in you experiencing the emotions of stress, anger fear and jealousy, preventing you from flourishing in life.

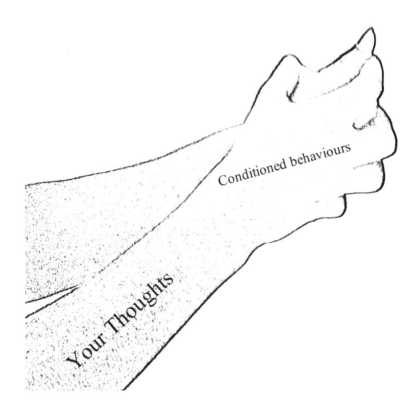

Conditioned behaviours

Your Thoughts

TRAPPED IN A PRISON – ANGER, FEAR, ANXIETY, STRESS, & SELFISH - STRUGGLE & SUFFERING

This picture depicts your conditioned behaviours (right hand) completely overwhelming the pure unconditioned true being (left arm). This is like a façade, concealing the uncorrupted true being and inhibiting it from expressing the true form.

Mere realisation or awareness of your conditioned behaviour, allows you to escape from your trap of conditioning, which allows you to thrive in boundless joy and experience life completely. You are once again the pure uncorrupted being, as you were when you were born. The intelligence (energy) flows through you, and you are finally free.

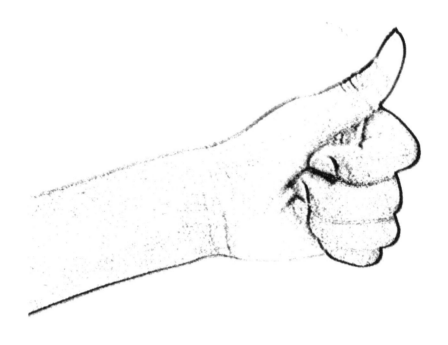

FREEDOM AGAIN

The Moment you are aware or conscious (mindful) of your thought which gives rise to your conditioned behaviour, at that moment the conditioned behaviour is dissolved. You have now emerged from that trap allowing that pure unconditioned uncorrupted innocent, enlightened being you once were to express and shine. Allow it to shine.

Only you can regain the missing space in your life…

Only you can access that intelligence...

Regain a life of mindfulness, consciousness, joy, creativity and freedom...

In this moment. NOW.

Acknowledgments:

I am grateful to my wife and children for their unrelenting support and love, without which this book would not have happened.

I am so grateful to the various human and other forms which include my family, my friends, my acquaintances, my teachers and all others who came into my life and helped me knowingly or unknowingly shed light on my own ignorance and conditioning.

For my beloved parents, for their unconditional love, affection, blessings and most importantly for having provided me the platform for self-discovery, to whom I dedicate this book.

Finally, I am grateful and bow down before the intelligence, as it has made me realize that I cannot do anything alone and I need the support of that divine knowing. This book and every other thing in my life has happened all due to the profound intelligence.

I remain grateful.

Other books by Santosh Nambiar:
A New Way of Living: One simple step to a life without Fear
Published by Balboa Press (HAY HOUSE) USA

Life a Meditation: Practical Pointers to Presence > Space > Peace
Published by LM Publication Australia

Is This It: Taking your life from Mediocrity to Creativity
Published by LM Publication Australia

"Taking your life from
Mediocrity to Creativity"

Is This It ?

SANTOSH NAMBIAR

Notes

Lightning Source UK Ltd.
Milton Keynes UK
UKHW01f0629010818
326613UK00001B/208/P